The Waltz Emperors

The Waltz Emperors

The Life and Times and Music of the Strauss Family

Joseph Wechsberg

Weidenfeld and Nicolson London

© Joseph Wechsberg 1973

Designed by Humphrey Stone
for George Weidenfeld and Nicolson Ltd
Printed and bound in Great Britain by
C. Tinling & Co., Warrington Road,
Prescot, Lancashire
Filmset by Keyspools Ltd, Golborne, Lancs.

ISBN 0 297 76594 9

For Ine

Contents

1
'Happy is he who forgets'

Legend and fact, myth and reality were always inseparably mixed up in the baroque city of Vienna – and in the story of the second Johann Strauss who remains, with Franz Schubert, the most Viennese among the many great composers who lived and worked there. For a long time the Strauss legend was perpetuated by admiring biographers who dedicated their efforts to the master. Strauss was too diffident to accept their eulogies. 'Unfortunately I didn't find time to read your book,' he wrote to Ludwig Eisenberg in 1894. He had been told the reviews were good. 'What better can you ask for?' In a moment of guilt he adds a postscript, 'May Heaven bring success to your work!' A kind-hearted man, always afraid to hurt people.

The image of Strauss, the fiddling, carefree, happy-go-lucky waltz king is as untrue as the legend of the Viennese as a people of 'fiddlers and dancers', gay and light-hearted. The great Viennese poets-and-moralists, a peculiarly Viennese mixture, always understood the undercurrents of sadness and melancholy in the hearts of the Viennese: Grillparzer, Raimund, Nestroy, Schnitzler, Hofmannsthal, Ödön von Horvath were conscious of it. The undertone of sadness is in the haunting songs of Schubert and the 'ecstatic' waltzes of Johann Strauss. The Viennese called them *Verzückungswalzer*, but ecstasy was always followed by sorrow, and they knew it. Berlioz said that Strauss's waltzes, with their melodies resembling a call of love, made him deeply sad. Many people sense the tear between the *joie de vivre* rhythm. Strauss loved Vienna, and when he wrote his finest melodies, he was, perhaps subconsciously, aware of the beginning of the end. Strauss was a musical poet, ahead of his time.

He was a true child of Vienna. The Viennese have always been able to overcome their sorrow and sadness and go on living. '*On ne vit qu'une fois*', you live only once, Strauss wrote to his third wife, Adele. His letters reveal him as a man of many fears and phobias, sensitive and

OPPOSITE The second Johann Strauss at his desk in the house at Bad Ischl.

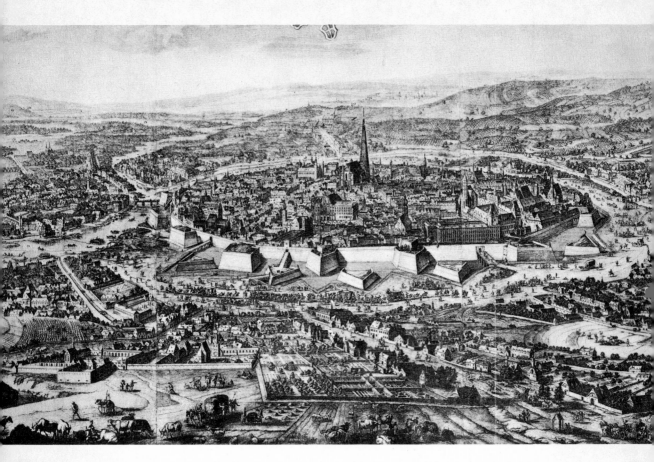

A view of Vienna at the beginning of the nineteenth century.

often insecure of himself. But there is nothing of this in his music, which has given millions of people a sense of happiness and exhilaration. That he was able to overcome his ever-present *Angst* in order to make people forget their anxieties for a short while makes him a very 'modern' composer, and explains his appeal today all over the world.

Strauss is said to owe much to Schubert who personifies the Viennese *genius loci*. Wine, women and song. *Lilac Time*. Live and let live. But Schubert was a deeply unhappy man. In 1824, when he was only twenty-seven, he wrote to his friend, the painter Leopold Kupelwieser, 'Imagine a man whose health will never be right again, and who in sheer despair over this makes things worse, instead of better . . . a man whose most brilliant hopes have perished.' At that time he wrote some of his greatest songs. He never overcame the dark abyss of his soul; the darkness is there, in his music, if you listen with your inner ear.

I feel that Strauss is much closer to another Austrian genius whose work was not as well known then as now – Joseph Haydn, born almost a century before Strauss. Haydn loved folk melodies and the popular songs of his native land; he often used Hungarian,

Croatian and Slav melodies in the fast movements of his string quartets and symphonies. Strauss later used such melodies in his dances. The great csárdás in *Die Fledermaus* is accepted even by one-hundred-and-ten-per-cent Hungarians. Haydn remains the optimist among the great composers; he believed in love and life, the beauty of nature and the sound of laughter. The inner tension in his music is always resolved in the happy ending – something even the divine Mozart did not always do. Haydn's music leaves us with an aftertaste of cheerfulness: so does a great Strauss waltz because Strauss too believed in love and life.

Haydn explained the secret of his music in 1802 in a letter to the members of the Musikverein on the small Baltic island of Rügen:

Often a secret voice whispered to me, 'There are so few happy and contented people here below; grief and sorrow are always their lot; perhaps your labours will once be a source from which the care-worn, or the man burdened with affairs, can derive a few moments' rest and refreshment.'

This is exactly what Johann Strauss tried to do. Once he instructed

The house in Vienna where Schubert lived.

his brother Eduard who conducted the Strauss orchestra to make his programmes 'not too serious'.

The public attends a Strauss concert hoping to be transported into a happy mood. Sometimes the people in the expensive boxes may not like the music but the galleries like it, *Vox populi, vox Dei*. People want to have fun, to be entertained, as at the theatre.

Strauss's letters reveal him as an often naive, sometimes complex man, very honest, loyal to his friends, with a genuine sense of humour, and able to laugh at himself. He never pretended. He never tried to avoid reality. Many Viennese escape out of the depressing reality into a beautiful dreamworld. Strauss helped to create this dreamworld but he himself never lived in it. When a Paris publisher asked him to write his biography, he declined. He had much in common with his contemporary, Giuseppe Verdi (twelve years older than Strauss) who refused to write his memories. 'Isn't it enough that people have to listen to my music? Why should they be forced to read my prose?' The two composers, so different in their origin and life work, had much in common as men and artists. Both went through a revolutionary youth; both became national heroes.

When the Viennese prepared the celebrations for the fiftieth anniversary of Johann Strauss, G. Hercevizi of *Neues Wiener Journal* went to see Verdi in Sant' Agata to ask him for a few words about the Viennese composer. Verdi smiled. 'I am sorry for Signor Strauss. His enthusiastic admirers will devour him. I admire him as a highly gifted colleague. The best I can wish him is good health. He will need it. To be called Strauss and have a jubilee in Vienna – may God help him!'

Strauss's universality, his wide appeal to heterogeneous groups was often misunderstood by narrow-minded esoterics. Once he said, 'If an operetta should become really popular, there must be something in it for everybody's taste. . . . The people in the gallery must get something they can easily remember and take home. They have no money to buy the piano score, let alone a piano.' Strauss was immediately accused of 'writing for the gallery', as though this were highly unethical. He reminded his critics that Mozart had not scorned to write for the galleries. Beethoven had, and *Fidelio* was a failure in its early productions. The wise old man in Sant' Agata understood this well. Once he told the young Giulio Gatti-Casazza who later became general manager of the Metropolitan Opera House:

Read the newspapers as little as possible but read most attentively the reports of the box office. These, whether you like it or not, are the only documents which measure success or failure. . . . If the public comes, the object is attained. If not – no. The theatre is intended to be full and not empty. That is something you must always remember.

Some of the finest music would not have been written if the composers had thought only of the critics and the snobs in the expensive stalls. Long live the gallery!

Being often insecure in his work, Strauss paid far too much attention to the critics. That is always dangerous in Vienna where criticism is often based on personal motives rather than artistic grounds. After the failure of *Ritter Pasman*, his only opera, at the Vienna Court Opera, Strauss was overjoyed when Wilhelm Jahn, the *Operndirektor*, decided to produce *Die Fledermaus* at Vienna's great opera house. Jahn wisely scheduled the performance to take place two weeks after Strauss's fiftieth jubilee in 1894, celebrating his debut in 1844. The premiere, on 28 October 1894, was a great success, with Marie Renard, Marie Lehmann (the sister of Lilli) and Ernest van Dyck. Strauss was to have conducted but he felt ill, and J.N.Fuchs took over, doing very well. The critics were enthusiastic. Some preferred to forget that they had badly panned *Die Fledermaus* twenty years earlier, after the original premiere. Since then, Strauss's masterpiece has become a world-wide success.

Yet also in 1894 Johann Strauss, in a letter to his brother, wrote, incredibly, 'If *Die Fledermaus* should remain an attraction at the Opera, I would refine (*verfeinern*) the score and permit its performance only at opera houses.' Some of Europe's great musical minds – Brahms, Bruckner, Mahler, Wagner, Berlioz, Nikisch, Goldmark, Anton Rubinstein, Ernst Schuch, and many others – had told Strauss how much they loved his work, and now he thought of 'refining' the perfect score! Fortunately he never touched it. '*Die Fledermaus* remains a musical comedy of the highest quality, today as new as on its first day, one of the few genuinely comic operas we Germans own since *Figaro*', wrote his biographer Heinrich Eduard Jacob.

But Strauss had not learned his lesson. He was seventy when Emperor Franz Joseph I attended a performance of the Strauss operetta *Der Zigeunerbaron*, and summoned the composer to his box. Afterwards Strauss reported the conversation to a friend: '"My dear Strauss," the Kaiser said, "I liked your opera. Really, very much."' Strauss waited a moment to let this sink in. 'Imagine, "opera", the Kaiser said. Opera!'

Each generation takes a different view of an artist's work. Johann Strauss is the exception. He was spared the bewildering ups and downs of popular favour. He was beloved during his life and he has been loved ever since. As an artist he is not problematical. As a man he is often contradictory.

While he made millions of people delirious with his music, he was often worried and depressed. He had a morbid horror of sickness and death. He was unable to attend the funeral of his beloved mother, and of his first wife with whom he spent some happy years. He was frightened by the very sight, even from a distance, of a hospital or a cemetery. He was afraid of draughts and suffered from neuralgia. High mountains and tunnels made him uncomfortable. When he took the train crossing the Semmering, a high mountain ridge near Vienna, he would draw the curtains of his compartment and sit down on the floor. This is the genius who expresses supreme *joie de vivre* in his music, who wrote the exuberant melody of 'Happy is he who forgets what cannot be changed'. One of his biographers writes that Strauss's veins 'were filled with bubbling champagne'. Nonsense. His veins were filled with blood, as ours, and his heart with everpresent fears, as ours. But he forced himself to overcome his fears to give his fellow beings happiness and joy. People feel this instinctively when they listen to his music. It is the deeper reason that he has never been out of fashion. Strauss was, and is, needed.

The members of the Strauss dynasty do not facilitate the biographer's task by their ways of life and work. All of them – Johann Strauss Father and his three sons, Josef, Eduard and the great

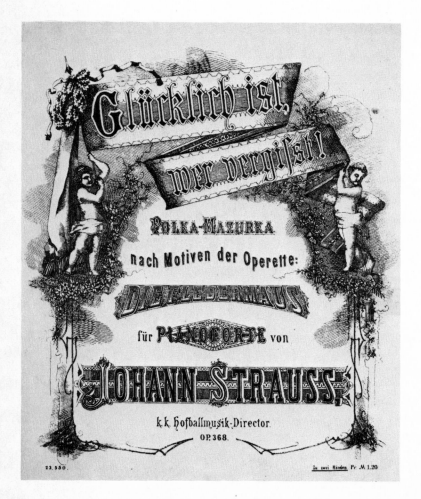

The title page of 'Happy is he who forgets' from the operetta, *Die Fledermaus*.

Johann – had a hectic profession which completely occupied them, much of the day and part of the night. They had no Boswell, no Eckermann following them around; they kept no diary; they were disorderly people. Many of their manuscripts have disappeared. They never took themselves seriously. Some artists are so certain of their immortality that they prepare for it consciously but not the Strausses. The younger Johann would never even think of posterity because such thoughts might conflict with his deep fear of death. Working in a highly extrovert profession, constantly surrounded by people, he remained a shy introvert in his private life. When Eduard Hanslick, the feared critic of the *Neue Freie Presse* and the city's musical pope, once asked Strauss to write his memoirs, Strauss gave a shrug and said, 'I've tried to dictate something to Adele but it was impossible. . . . Really I couldn't do it.'

Apart from his music Strauss left few documents and records. Most of his letters were kept by his third wife who made a narrow selection when she published some of them; many were lost during the last war when the Nazis requisitioned all material left by Strauss. There is also the long preface he did for the Breitkopf & Härtel edition of his father's works. The first English-language biography of the Strauss dynasty was published only in 1939. And the first volume of the collected works of the second Johann Strauss was published in Vienna only in the summer of 1967 – just one hundred years after the first performance of *The Blue Danube*. An excellent catalogue of works for the first Strauss was compiled by Max Schönherr and Karl Reinöhl, containing the case history of each work, numbered from 1 to 251. No similar catalogue has yet been published about the work of the more famous son.

In 1936, the Johann Strauss Society was founded in Vienna but two years later, after the *Anschluss*, the Nazis forbade all activities on behalf of Strauss when serious doubts arose about his Aryan descent. In 1945 the Strauss Society was revived. Professor Fritz Racek began to collect and edit the composer's collected works. His task has been frustrating, to say the least. Many of Johann Strauss's sketches, scores, letters, and memoranda have disappeared. Of his 450-odd dance and stage compositions, less than 30 exist in autograph. (By comparison, many of Lanner's works exist in the original; he wrote with meticulous care and looked after his manuscripts. Many of Father Strauss's manuscripts survive; he wrote fast, often in visible haste. Of Josef's manuscripts, almost none exist.)

During the first thirty years of his career, when the second Johann Strauss wrote most of his dance compositions, he was always under pressure. He might have to deliver a new waltz for a big ball at night, having signed a contract long ago, and sometimes he would not have

even started work in the morning. He was invariably late. Often the copyists would be waiting in the next room while Strauss was trying to finish his new composition. Sometimes three or more copyists worked simultaneously on several parts of a waltz. As soon as they had a few pages ready, they would take them to the musicians who were in another room nearby. The musicians would start practising their parts. Professor Racek found several orchestra scores of waltzes by the elder Strauss sliced with a razor blade so that several copyists could work on one page of the score at the same time. Finally, the composer-conductor would join his orchestra for the first rehearsal. It was almost always a race against the clock, and most members of the Strauss family paid a high price for it by wrecking their health.

There was always much movement and often considerable long-distance travel. Today many artists become victims of the jet age; they travel too much and too fast and ruin themselves prematurely. But in the 1830s and 1840s, the elder Strauss took his orchestra all over Europe, in horse-drawn coaches. His sons made many trips to Russia.

Success meant expansion. At one time the Strauss organization had
over two hundred employees – musicians, copyists, coachmen, ushers,
bookkeepers, administrative personnel. But apparently no one had the
task of looking after the scores and putting them in a safe place. No
one had much respect for the composer's handwritten manuscripts.
Tonight or tomorrow he would probably write another one. It was
pretty late in his career when Adele, Johann's third wife, began to keep
his manuscripts together and to organize his work. She would keep
paper and pencils in each room in case Strauss had a sudden idea. He
always had ideas, day and night, sometimes even in his dreams; in the
morning he would play a melody for his wife, and write it down. He
never had to wait for ideas, he never laboriously developed them.
They seemed to fly towards him, rays of musical sunshine. It is hard
to understand how many people during his time in Vienna could
believe the malicious rumours that he had used ideas left by his gifted
brother Josef. Johann had no need of anyone's ideas. Also, he would
never have done it. He had a high sense of professional ethics. After

working for a quarter of a century on the Johann Strauss edition, Fritz Racek has found 'not a trace of evidence that Johann Strauss ever used any material that wasn't his own'.

Another persistent rumour claimed that he had specialists to orchestrate his works. Even the devoted Eisenberg writes after *Das Spitzentuch der Königin*, in 1880, 'Strauss, who wasn't quite at home when he started orchestrating his operettas, now attained complete independence.' That was six years after Strauss had finished the magnificent score of *Die Fledermaus*. Eisenberg also wrote that Richard Genée, Strauss's able librettist, had 'taken part in the technical execution of the musical work'. Was he cautiously referring to local gossip that Strauss needed help? Ernst Decsey who wrote the best Strauss biography, after much thorough research states flatly, 'The only ones who helped Strauss – mechanically, so to speak – were Kupfer, the copyist of Brahms, and Kraus, a viola player in Eduard Strauss's orchestra.' Both worked only as copyists. In 1894, Johann Strauss wrote to his friend, the publisher Gustav Lewy, 'No dance composition of mine was published that I didn't score myself.' Referring to a certain request, he continued, 'I cannot make an exception. This is a matter of artistic integrity.'

Strauss rigorously refused to give unfinished scores to theatre managers who had scheduled rehearsals and needed the music, 'even if it's unfinished – our men can do that at the theatre'. The answer was always no. Strauss was a master of orchestration; in his younger years he had arranged such complicated works as Wagner's *Tristan und Isolde* and *Parsifal* for his orchestra. Wagner and Brahms, two great masters of instrumentation who rarely agreed on anything, both expressed admiration for the scores of Johann Strauss. Max Reger, a master of polyphony, paid tribute to Strauss in his Ballet Suite, Opus 130. Max Hasse, his biographer, writes that Reger, always searching for the ideally light texture of his orchestra sound 'occasionally came close to Johann Strauss, his refined instrumentation and delicacy of orchestration, Strauss's ability to create with simple means beautiful colours and a sort of floating gracefulness.' Real musicians never believed the rumours that were the result of intrigue and backstage gossip, typical of the city of Vienna.

Much of the gossip directed against Strauss had its source in a recurrent Viennese phenomenon. Unusually gifted people were always attacked in Vienna, then and now. Genius was considered 'dangerous', mediocrity was 'safe'. The Austrian bureaucracy, powerful since 1526, when the Habsburg Archduke Ferdinand crushed the mutiny of the burghers and lower nobility in Vienna and replaced the city fathers with appointed civil servants, has always been suspicious of talent and greatness. Vienna's poets, since Grillparzer, Raimund and Nestroy, learned the bitter truth – and so did the great composers, from Gluck and Mozart to Schœnberg and Berg. Long after Mahler was recognized in Western Europe and America, much of his work was practically unknown in Vienna; the first complete cycle of Mahler's works was performed there in 1967. Schœnberg's masterpiece, *Moses and Aaron*, was first performed in 1962 at the Vienna State Opera – by a guest company of Berlin's German Opera. To be completely accepted in Vienna it helps to be dead.

Even Strauss, one of the most beloved composers, had his problems. Some critics accused him of 'monopolizing the local dance music'. One of them wrote, 'The activities of Herr Strauss are limited by constantly repeating his own thoughts, and his new pro-

JOHANN STRAUSS, DER WALZERKÖNIG.

Theo Zasche's cartoon of Strauss as the Waltz King, drawn in 1899.

ducts are often copies of the older ones.' Others reprimanded him for his 'noisy, baroque instrumentation', and 'mixing up the most heterogeneous elements so that the dance rhythm disappears'. Some admitted 'the wealth of his melodies' but censured 'his typical Austrian superficiality'. His conducting was compared to 'a fencing lesson, set to music'.

Fritz Lange, one of the admiring biographers, admits that some of Johann Strauss's early compositions 'show nervous haste'. He is quite right. After 1844, when Strauss had his own orchestra, he often worked in a hurry, writing utility music – waltzes, polkas, gallops for dancers. It is hard to believe that he wrote the complex score of *Die Fledermaus* in forty-two nights, unless one remembers that Rossini needed only thirteen days for *Il Barbiere di Siviglia*, one of the great all-time comic masterpieces, and that Donizetti wrote *Don Pasquale* in eleven days.

The original score of *Die Fledermaus* (kept by Fritz Racek in an old-fashioned safe in his office at the Vienna City Hall) is done with astonishing care. Strauss used a steel pen, writing in black ink. Only very occasionally are there erasures. The melodies are almost always clearly written; probably they were first sketched out. The accompaniments are finished down to the last detail. There is clarity of the texture throughout. Sometimes Strauss does not write out several bars, but draws the vertical lines and writes in coloured pencil, A, B, C, D, referring to an earlier, similar phrase. Creative haste must not be confused with superficiality. Verdi finished the score of *Rigoletto* in forty days. Often he never bothered to write out the accompaniment, leaving the details for later. The handwriting of *'La donna è mobile'* gives the impression of having been written in great haste yet it has remained one of the most popular melodies ever written. Genius may break all rules.

Though Strauss seemed to create with facility, he was always involved in the creative process, thinking of his work subconsciously all the time, awake or asleep. When the melodies had formed in his mind, he would dash them off. All his life he remained under the musical influence of his father. Even in some early works, with their hastily done, unimaginative orchestration, there is sometimes a sudden flash of genius, and always a sense of youth and freshness. They are immensely alive; and they remain alive, after 120 years.

Later on, the son began to sense his father's limitations, a certain dryness and shortness, caused by insufficient length of phrase. The father would often substitute rhythm when he ran out of melody. The son discovered what every great composer must discover for himself: the secret of the long melody. In this respect he resembles the Italians. Verdi sometimes prepares the listener with a few hm-ta-ta-ta bars for some of his greatest melodies. Strauss artfully prepares his public, dancing or listening, with a few hm-ta-ta (*one*-two-three) for the cantilena that follows.

With the creative artist's God-given instinct the younger Strauss sensed that he had overtaken the beloved father, as he extended the limits. Sooner or later, the inevitable comparisons were made. In Vienna, then a city of 400,000 people, there were 400,000 waltz experts. All Viennese considered themselves co-owners of the Strausses, just as now they consider themselves joint proprietors of another beloved institution, the Vienna State Opera. Many of them never go there but they all have their ideas how it should be run. The Strauss family were criticized and praised; and they were always told how to do it.

The great waltzes which Johann Strauss Son wrote after 1860 – 'concert' or 'symphonic' waltzes – were masterpieces of musical structure and musical invention. They begin with an introduction that sets the mood and end with a coda, often a nostalgic last glance back. In between there are five parts, each part with two skilfully contrasted melodies. Strauss wrote some 160 waltzes, leaving over sixteen hundred musical ideas in these works – not to mention all the other things he wrote. His career is one long successful experiment.

He worked carefully on his great waltzes. He would study the number of bar groups in a phrase, and he re-wrote constantly. Only the twelfth revision of the 'truffle couplet' from *Das Spitzentuch der Königin* left him satisfied. This is an extreme case, but not an exception. Musicologists have compared Johann Strauss to his contemporary, Sir Arthur Sullivan, also a meticulous craftsman. Sometimes he would change details in the original scores when he looked through them before they were printed. He had second thoughts and wanted to improve the music; he may have felt that there was something done too quickly in the early manuscript. Sometimes it has become impossible to ascertain which is the definitive version, but Racek is convinced that no one else was permitted to make such changes.

After the death of Strauss in 1899, his widow kept all his possessions, including his musical manuscripts. Unfortunately Strauss never bothered to catalogue his works. The original manuscripts often disappeared among copyists, musicians, souvenir hunters. Once Brahms asked Strauss through a mutual friend, the writer Max Kalbeck, for a few pages from the score of Strauss's only opera, *Ritter Pasman*. Strauss wrote to Kalbeck, 'With regard to the manuscripts which Brahms wants I looked in my drawers and couldn't find a single page. As you know, I am not used to keeping manuscripts. Adele owns part of *Der Zigeunerbaron*. I remember that I tore out of the *Pasman* score the end of the first act.'

Brahms with Strauss's third wife, Adele.

When Adele Strauss died, in 1926, her daughter Alice Meyszner inherited the collection. There was also a second collection of Strauss manuscripts and memorabilia that had been compiled by Adele's brother-in-law, the Viennese banker Josef Simon. He left it to his widow, Luise, who continued to collect what she could find. Unfortunately neither collection contains some important Strauss works which have disappeared.

After Hitler's invasion of Austria the Gestapo requisitioned the Alice Meyszner Collection and the Luise Simon Collection. In the following years Hitler and Goering became noted 'art collectors'. Goebbels was said to be particularly interested in the original score of *Die Fledermaus*.

After the end of the war, the Strauss collections, 'Aryanized property', were gradually returned to the legal heirs. Alice Meyszner had died in 1945, Luise Simon the following year. The heirs lived in Switzerland, England, Mexico. After years of complicated negotiations, the City of Vienna purchased a considerable part of the collections from various heirs. In 1962, the City administration acquired the original score of *Die Fledermaus* at an auction held by Karl und Faber in Munich, for 167,900 marks (over $40,000). The score is now part of the permanent Johann Strauss Collection at the Music Library in the City Hall. Thus ends the last chapter in the strange, long history of Johann Strauss's masterpiece.

The Strauss Collection contains the autograph scores of almost all operettas and about thirty dance compositions by Johann Strauss, some fifty by his father, and several by Joseph Lanner; a complete collection of first editions of the works of these composers and of Josef Strauss; letters, programmes, sketches, portraits, pictures, and many caricatures drawn by Strauss.

Eventually, the complete edition of the Strauss works will have fifty volumes: the dance compositions in chronological sequence, the operettas, the opera *Ritter Pasman*, the pasticcio *Wiener Blut*, the ballet *Aschenbrödel*, various compositions for voice and for chorus, and other fragments. 'There is hope,' concludes Fritz Racek, the editor, 'that this complete edition will help us to rediscover some beautiful, now forgotten works by Johann Strauss.'

2

How it began: the first Strauss and Lanner

The Strauss dynasty, now firmly associated with the glory of Vienna, did not originate from there; most Viennese have their ancestry elsewhere and a fine distinction is still made between a 'born' Viennese and a 'learned' one. A few years ago, Professor Hanns Jäger-Sunstenau, historian and archivist of the City of Vienna, after much scientific research, published his findings in *Johann Strauss, der Walzerkönig und seine Dynastie*. He traced the family back to one Wolf Strauss, possibly born in the early eighteenth century in Ofen, the old part of Budapest. Wolf's son Johann Michael Strauss was born in Ofen in 1720. It is not certain when the family moved to Vienna but Johann Michael was certainly married there for the certificate appears on page 210 of the wedding book no. 60 of St Stephen's Cathedral. According to the registration, Johann Michael, a 'baptized Jew', the son of Wolf and Theresia Strauss, 'both Jewish', married Rosalia Buschinin on 11 February 1762. He was employed as a servant to Field-Marshal Lieutenant Count von Roggendorff, who had been active during the Seven Years' War.

This written proof that the great great grandfather of the famous Strauss was a Jew caused great embarrassment to the Nazis. Jäger-Sunstenau and some other genealogists had discovered the entry in 1935. After Austria's *Anschluss* in 1938, all the scholars who were known to have looked at the wedding book were summoned together and told to keep 'strict silence' about their research if they knew what was good for them. No wonder, says Jäger-Sunstenau:

If the ancestry of the family Strauss had become known, it would have been a catastrophe for the entire music business in the Third Reich. All Strauss melodies would have to be banned, like the beautiful music of Mendelssohn-Bartholdy and many others. Imagine what that would have done to the repertory in concerts and radio. And it would have been a calamity for the notorious *Stürmer*. Its posters everywhere said, 'The world

OPPOSITE A colour lithograph of the elder Johann Strauss by Kriehuber.

OVERLEAF A tavern scene, painted by Neder, which would have been the childhood background of the first Strauss.

24

knows Johann Strauss, the waltz king, with his uncomparable melodies. There is probably no other music which is so German and so close to the nation as that of the great waltz king. . . . Jewish legacy hunters are to blame for the fact that his own descendants now live in poverty. . . .'

Johann Strauss never had any descendants. The 'legacy hunter' had been his widow Adele, who was Jewish, and was his legal heir. The true story, if it became known, would be truly shocking for the *Stürmer*, however. In order to prevent this, the Hitler regime committed 'a grotesque forgery' which Jäger-Sunstenau and others revealed after the end of the regime. Not unexpectedly, the Nazis worked with astonishing thoroughness.

The wedding book no. 60 of St Stephen's in Vienna was confiscated and sent to the *Reichssippenamt* in Berlin. There the book was photographed page by page and a photocopy was made. On page 1 the conformity of original and photo copy was officially certified on 20 February 1941.

Original and copy were returned to Vienna. The original wedding book was hidden in the vaults of the super-secret Haus-, Hof- und Staatsarchiv. The copy was handed over to the authorities at St Stephen's.

'The expert who looked at the copy knew at once what had happened,' says Jäger-Sunstenau. 'The Strauss entry had disappeared from the page. And the name Strauss had also vanished from the index page 361.'

The aim was reached: the uncomfortable Strauss item could no longer be seen, and Strauss music, so very German, as the *Stürmer* had written, could be broadcast all over the Third Reich. To attain such a noble aim it was only just and fair, by the ten valid standards, to forge some old documents.

After the Liberation, the original wedding book was returned to St Stephen's where they still keep the falsified copy.

Johann Michael Strauss died at the age of eighty in a Viennese old people's home in 1800. His oldest son, Franz, became a tavern keeper around 1804. He married Barbara Dollman whose father had been an employee of the Imperial Riding School. They had a daughter Ernestine and a son Johann Baptist, who was to be a great waltz composer himself and father of the waltz king. Johann Baptist was born on 14 March 1804 on the second floor of the Strauss tavern, The Good Shepherd. Romantic biographers have speculated that Schubert and Beethoven may have been among the habitués in Flossgasse No. 7. No proof exists. Beethoven liked to walk in the nearby Prater and sometimes he amused himself playing the piano at the Eisvogel, a popular establishment. Little is known about Johann's early years. He was seven when his mother died of 'the creeping fever' and one year later the tavern-keeper married Katharina Feldberger. Five years

OPPOSITE A watercolour by Rudolf von Alt of St Stephen's Cathedral, where Johann Michael Strauss married Rosalie Buschinin in 1762.

ABOVE Franz Strauss, a tavern keeper, and father of the elder Johann Strauss.

RIGHT Number 7 Flossgasse, the birthplace of the elder Strauss, in a watercolour by Zajicek.

later his father was found dead in the Danube. It is not known whether it was an accident or whether Strauss had committed suicide in a moment of depression. He was known to suffer from long spells of melancholia and he had financial problems: after his death there were large unpaid debts to brewers' draymen. The children's stepmother soon married a certain Golder. They were still very poor. Katharina was not pleased when Schani, as the family called Johann, was always hanging around the tavern, watching the itinerant musicians who had come from the Danube boats.

Strauss begged his stepfather Golder to buy him a small Bavarian fiddle, and when he got it he practised a lot. Many biographers repeat the anecdote that he would pour beer into his violin 'to improve its dry sound'. The most one can say is that this method was never tried in Cremona where they knew all about violins. Johann loved playing the violin. Nothing else mattered. His formal education was sketchy, a few years in grammar school. Much later, when Johann Strauss mingled with emperors and queens, he regretted his lack of education, and decided that his sons should have it better.

When he was twelve, he was sent as apprentice to a bookbinder named Lichtscheidl, said to be *ein seelensguter Mensch*, the very soul of a man. This did not prevent him from beating up the boy when he made a mistake. Johann spent five unhappy years there.

One day he had had enough and ran away, with his fiddle. He did not get very far. He fell asleep in a meadow near Kahlenberg. A friend of his parents, a musician named Polischansky, found him there and took him home. Polischansky was the boy's only teacher. Only after Strauss had become famous, did he study composition with Ignaz von Seyfried, a friend of Beethoven, and violin with Leopold Jansa – in secret. When Strauss was fifteen, he joined Michael Pamer's orchestra and met Joseph Lanner.

Lanner was the first of the waltz composers. He wrote his earliest waltzes when the older Johann was still practising on his small violin. Joseph Lanner was born on 12 April 1801, in the St Ulrich district (now Neubau), a short walk from the Imperial Palace. His early musical development is intimately connected with that of Johann Strauss. Both lived in a world of their own that was filled with music. Lanner's father, Martin Lanner, was a glovemaker, a fairly well-to-do burgher who worked for many rich and aristocratic customers. Joseph wanted no part of his father's business; he wanted to be a musician. He learned to play the violin by looking at others. As a composer he was also a complete autodidact. He was truly gifted though. Only in recent times people are beginning to take Lanner's full measure.

At the age of fourteen, Lanner joined the popular dance orchestra of Michael Pamer (1782–1827), a talented composer now remembered for his *Linzerische Tänze*, a mixture of *ländler* and early waltzes. Pamer was a well known Viennese character. He was nearly always pleasantly drunk. Once he wrote a waltz as a homage to his favourite beer, made by the Hütteldorf Brewery. After the coda, he would empty a half-litre glass of beer, in front of the audience. The delighted people would cheer and ask him to repeat the waltz. Sometimes it was repeated twelve times which meant drinking over a gallon of beer. (The brewery, delighted with the publicity, provided Pamer with un-limited supplies.) When too much beer interfered with Pamer's activities as a composer, he would ask his young violinist, Lanner, 'to write something'. At night the orchestra would perform Lanner's waltzes. No credit was given to the teenage composer.

Eventually Lanner got tired of working for Pamer. In 1818, at the age of seventeen, he formed his own band with Karl and Johann Drahanek, good musicians whose family had come from Bohemia. The trio – two violins and a guitar – would appear at the Green Huntsman in Leopoldstadt and in Jüngling's Kaffeehaus. Lanner was composing, and, at last, able to announce his own pieces.

Soon after Lanner formed his trio with the Drahaneks, he asked Strauss to join them as viola player; later, he also hired a cellist. Lanner was 'much older' – three years, to be exact and Johann admired him very much.

The Lanner Quintet often performed in the Prater. It was probably the first outdoor orchestra there. They also played at Das Rebhuhn (The Partridge) near St Stephen's, which existed until a few years ago when it became a pizzeria. Schubert and his friend, the painter Moritz von Schwind, would often come there to listen to the music. After performing a few pieces one of the Drahanek boys would take a tin plate and make a collection around the tables.

Lanner, flaxen-haired, and dark-haired Strauss became close friends. For some time they lived in a room in Windmühlgasse 18, sharing their girls, their debts and their shirts, and producing fine material for later generations of scenario writers. According to a much repeated story, they were once down to their last common shirt. One wore it, and the shirtless one stayed at home.

Lanner's first publisher was Anton Diabelli who commissioned the Beethoven variations which bear his name; his second was Tobias Haslinger. Both were shrewd businessmen, but also their clients' friends. Beethoven and other composers were almost daily at Haslinger's place in Paternoster Street, around eleven in the morning; many had their letters sent there. Lanner and Strauss probably met Beethoven there, but neither recorded it.

In his early compositions Lanner adapted the simple eight-bar waltz phrases of the Danube river boat musicians. He was strongly influenced by Weber; in *Die Schönbrunner*, one of his finest waltzes, he uses the D flat major motif from *The Invitation to the Dance*. Popular demand forced Lanner to enlarge his quintet into a string orchestra in 1824, and later he divided it, at the same time adding wind and percussion instruments. He conducted one part of the orchestra and put his friend Strauss in charge of the other one.

Dual management always breeds trouble and the inevitable happened. The Viennese public, always delighted to play two prima donnas against each other (the latest instance is Bernstein *v.* Karajan) became divided in *Lannerianer* and *Straussianer*. There were the usual, predictable rumours. It was whispered that Lanner had performed Strauss waltzes under his name, and that Strauss had taken girls from Lanner. The official break-up occurred in 1825 after a regular free-for-all on the musicians' platform at the Schwarzer Bock, a popular dance hall in the Wieden district. There was much excitement, the newspapers wrote about it, and the event received its musical stamp when Lanner wrote his *Trennungswalzer* (Separation Waltz), Opus 19. No one was surprised. In Vienna during the waltz age all emotions were expressed in waltz themes. Lanner's waltz is early programme music, with sounds of a drunken brawl and people's hiccups. The two friends made up again when Lanner married Franziska Jahns in 1828. Later they often met and played each other's music.

In the image:

Sonntag 9. Jänner
Oeffentlicher Ball.

Montag 10. Jänner
Gesellschaftsball d. H. M.

Dinstag 11. Jänner

Mittwoch 12. Jänner
Gesellschaftsball d. H. F.

Donnerstag 13. Jänner

Samstag 15. Jänner

Sonntag 16. Jänner
Oeffentlicher Ball.

Montag 17. Jänner
Gesellschaftsball d. H. T.

Dinstag 18. Jänner
Industrie Elite Ball.

Mittwoch 19. Jänner
Gesellschaftsball d. H. La Roche.

Donnerstag 20. Jänner
Cerito Ball d. H. R. u. M.

Samstag 22. Jänner
Fantasie Ball d. H. R. u. M.

Sonntag 23. Jänner
Oeffentlicher Ball.

Montag 24. Jänner
Gesellschaftsball d. H. bildenden Künstler.

Dinstag 25. Jänner
Gesellschaftsball des B. C.

Mittwoch 26. Jänner
Gesellschaftsball des H. v. Webersfeld.

Donnerstag 27. Jänner
Cerito Ball d. H. R. u. M.

Samstag 29. Jänner
Fantasie Ball d. H. M. u. R.

Sonntag 30. Jänner
Oeffentlicher Ball.

Montag 31. Jänner
Benefice d. H. Lanner.

Dinstag 1. Februar
Fortuna Ball.

Mittwoch 2. Februar
bürgl. Artillerie.

Donnerstag 3. Februar
Cerito Ball des R. M.

Samstag 5. Februar
Fantasie Ball R. u. M.

Sonntag 6. Februar
Oeffentlicher Ball.

Montag 7. Februar
Grosser öffentl. Festball.

Dinstag 8. Februar

Kapellmeister u. Musikdirector
Jos. Lanner

Tanz Arrangeur
Hr. Webersfeld

Ball Eintheilung
für den Carneval 1842
in dem Saale
ZUR GOLDENEN BIRNE
auf der Landstrasse
Carl Hoer.

In 1829 Lanner was named *Hofballmusikdirektor* (director of music for court balls). At twenty-eight he had reached Vienna's highest official musical position. Lanner did not change, however. He remained a simple, lovable man, living quietly in a small house in the outskirts of the city. He hated to leave town and he was not happy when he had to go to Milan to conduct the orchestra at a court ball. He lived and died in Döbling, where Beethoven often walked the streets, brooding and scowling. Lanner was a man with few ambitions. He liked a glass of wine, his pipe, and the laughter of the woman he loved, while he walked in his room, writing down his 'improvisations', or playing the fiddle. But he worked too much; all waltz musicians did. During the *Fasching* (the carnival season), there were many balls. A prominent conductor was expected to compose a new waltz for each important ball, to rehearse and to conduct it. Lanner got tired and drank too much. Fritz Lange, his biographer, tells of a court ball at the Redoutensäle when Emperor Franz noticed that Lanner was slightly swaying while he conducted the orchestra. The Emperor asked Baron Kutschera, his Master of Ceremonies, 'to take out Lanner

ABOVE A programme of balls in the winter of 1842 to be conducted by Lanner at Die Goldene Birne.

OPPOSITE ABOVE The village of Döbling, near Vienna, where Lanner lived and died.

OPPOSITE BELOW A lithograph by Katzler of Lanner and Strauss in a coffee shop, standing to the right of the cashier. The actor and playwright Ferdinand Raimund is sitting in front of them with upraised arm.

or he might fall off the platform and hurt himself'. One night Lanner
made the mistake of showing his shirt, wet with perspiration, to the
Archduchess Sophie of Bavaria (who later became the formidable,
domineering mother of Emperor Franz Joseph I) to explain 'how hard
he had worked'. The prudish archduchess was not amused. The
Hofballmusikdirektor was fired.

The early compositions of Lanner and Strauss are similar in their
structure but both soon broke out of the simple one-two-three
pattern which they kept only in the accompaniment, while they
introduced new variations in the melody – syncopation, cross-
rhythms, surprising rests. In temperament Lanner and Strauss were
completely different. Lanner's waltzes were lyrical and melodious,
Strauss's were dramatic and exciting. Their music reflected their
personalities. Lanner, quiet, and blond; Strauss, elegant in a somewhat demoniac way, with his pale face, black hair, moustache.
Somebody called him 'Satan as a cavalier'.

Both reached maturity soon, as men and musicians, and each went
his way. Lanner remained shy and withdrawn, but there is often an
unexpected depth of feeling in his music. There is nothing demoniac
about Lanner but an occasional melancholy that gives his music a very
modern sound. He was deeply religious – like the pious Bruckner –
and began and ended his compositions with the words, 'With God'.
Lanner reflects the mood and the problems of his era, the Biedermeier.

The name Biedermeier is derived from *Biedermayers Liederlust*,
humorous poems published in the satirical weekly *Fliegende Blätter*.
Their fictitious author, Gottlieb Biedermayer, a naïve schoolteacher,

36

became synonymous with the era that began after the Congress of Vienna in 1815 and ended with the Revolution of 1848. Such labels are always vague. The Biedermeier became known as a time of middle-class cosiness and *Backhendl* prosperity (*Backhendl*, chicken fried in egg and breadcrumbs, is still a favourite with the Viennese and so is the young wine called Heuriger, 'this year's'.) There is a Biedermeier style in furniture, china, glassware, the legend of 'Old Vienna'; Schubert's *Dreimäderlhaus (Lilac Time)*. Ferdinand Raimund's fairy-tale plays, the waltzes of Lanner and the older Strauss.

In the autumn of 1830, the twenty-year-old Chopin came to Vienna to give some concerts. No one was interested and Chopin wrote home that 'Lanner, Strauss and their waltzes dominate everything'. Not everything though. Two years before Nicolò Paganini had created a sensation in Vienna and gave twenty concerts. Pastry cooks made petit fours in the shape of tiny violins, inns served Paganini goulash, and a chronicler wrote that Paganini 'even dethroned the giraffe which the Pasha of Egypt had just presented to the court'. The local composers quickly cashed in on the Paganini boom. Lanner wrote a *quodlibet* with Paganini melodies, and Strauss wrote the Paganini Waltz, Opus 11. Both performed Paganini compositions in their concerts. No one seemed to object; there were no copyright problems. A biographer wrote, 'One can imagine that Johann Strauss played the rondo not quite like Paganini, but the applause was

An advertisement for Liebig's meat extract.

Johan Strauß u. Josef Lanner
k.k. Hofball Musik Direktor.

Verstummt ist zwar der Meister Seitenspiel,
Das Tausende mit Heiterkeit durchdrungen
Und leicht beschwingt verfehlte nie sein Ziel,
Sobald der Seiten erster Ton erklungen.

Doch ihrer Weisen lebensfroher Sang,
Getragen auf des Frohsinns Aetherschwingen,
Wenn auch verstimmt der Meister Seitenklang,
Wird in der lieben Heimath nie verklingen.

terrific. . . . Now those who could not afford to listen to Paganini could hear his *alter ego* almost gratis since contributions "for the music" were voluntary'. Later, Franz Günzburg wrote, 'Strauss quickly sensed the new mood and had the good idea to introduce regular ticket prices, and Lanner, no fool, did the same'.

Richard Wagner, nineteen, came to Vienna in the summer of 1832. In *My Life* he wrote that he was 'very much at home in this lively city during a pleasant stay of six weeks':

I visited the theatres, heard Strauss, made excursions, and altogether had a very good time. I am afraid I contracted a few debts as well which I paid off later on when I was conductor in Dresden. . . . I shall never forget the extraordinary playing of Johann Strauss who put equal enthusiasm into everything he played, and very often made the audience almost frantic with delight. At the beginning of a new waltz this demon of the Viennese musical spirit shook like a Pythian priestess on the tripod, and veritable groans of ecstasy (which, without doubt, were more due to his music than to the drinks in which the audience had indulged) raised their worship for the magic violinist to almost bewildering heights of frenzy.

A shrewd though not always objective observer, Wagner called the waltz 'a more powerful drug than alcohol . . . the very first bars set the whole audience aflame'. Wagner had correctly sensed the mood of the Viennese. While Mozart, Beethoven and Schubert were often ignored, the people were ecstatic at the Kärntnerthortheater when the works of Rossini, Bellini and Donizetti were given. When Rossini came to Vienna in 1822, the 'local' composers were forgotten. Only the waltz craze continued. During the *Fasching* of 1832, a few months before Wagner's visit, there were 772 balls, attended by 200,000 people, half the population of Vienna, counting babies and old people. The big balls were the great events of the year. They were also social barriers. Tens of thousands of people would patiently wait for hours, 'held back by Austrian soldiers who could not even speak German', to see the arrival of the coaches with the beautiful people.

Twenty years after Wagner's first journey to Vienna, the oldest son of 'the magic violinist' repaid Wagner's admiration for his father when he began playing selections from Wagner's operas in his band concerts even before some of the operas were performed.

The 'powerful drug' of the waltz was effective not only in Vienna. In 1833 Strauss took his orchestra of thirty to Budapest, the following year to Dresden, Leipzig and Berlin. In Vienna, his admirers waited anxiously for news about his performances. It had long been said in Berlin that Strauss, that dance musician, 'had bewitched the crazy Viennese Phæacians', as though this could not happen in the more sober climate of Berlin. But the Strauss concerts in Berlin, some in the presence of the court and the visiting Czar of Russia, were a smash hit.

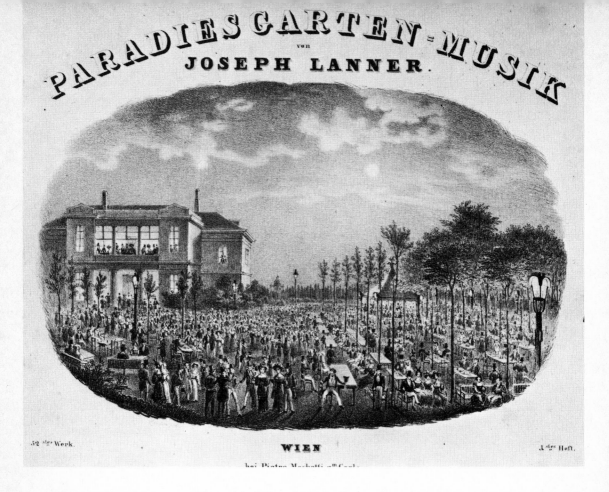

PARADIES GARTEN-MUSIK

von

JOSEPH LANNER.

WIEN

ABOVE The typical evening scene in one of Vienna's gardens, shown on the cover of Lanner's music.

The critic Eduard Maria Öttinger wrote in the Berlin *Figaro:*

Strauss is a musical phenomenon. He is the waltz personified, his compositions are bolts of lightning, musical bon mots. . . . His name was a magnet attracting a glamorous audience. The Empress and his Majesty the King graciously contributed their presence and their applause.

In Vienna, the *Straussianer* were delighted with the victory of their hero on a foreign battlefield. Yet some critics wondered whether Strauss could be called 'a veritable artist'. One quoted the famous diva Angelica Catalani who had said of a rival, Henriette Sontag, 'Elle est grande dans son genre mais son genre est petit'.

The Berlin success created unexpected problems. After Haslinger had published Johann Strauss's *Waltz Souvenir of Berlin*, Opus 78, a Berlin publisher named Müller published a waltz called *Souvenir de Berlin*, by Strauss, no first name. In Vienna this would have been impossible; everybody knew how Lanner and Strauss wrote. 'But in Germany, in France and even in America some people are cooking a little soup of their own on a fire by Strauss', a Viennese paper reported.

40

Vienna in the 1830s was not a dull place. Something was always going on, and people could have fun without spending much money. There were the merry-go-rounds in the Prater, the wax figures cabinet, at the 'Optik' one could see 'the most beautiful Alpine valleys', and nearby one could admire the Eskimo girls. There were flower exhibitions in the garden of Archduke Anton, and dances in every inn. At the Praterstern, Heinrich Schreier's monkey theatre was the great attraction. In the Brigittenau, crowds met on large meadows. 'Dozens of bands made a terrific noise, and at night there were fireworks.'

After a monster party that Johann Strauss gave in Baden, near Vienna, with outdoor concerts, a performance at the Kurpark, and a ball at the Redoute, the *Theaterzeitung* wrote on 4 September 1830, 'For this day everybody in Vienna had to come to Baden. One did not talk about politics. For twelve hours Strauss was the absolute ruler in spite of Metternich and the Emperor Franz.' People also rediscovered the simple pleasures of nature, walking in the Vienna Woods. In May 1834, the *Theaterzeitung* suggested that a nice excursion could be made to the Krapfenwald: 'For the comfort of the excursionists there are always saddled donkeys in Grinzing.' Strauss wrote his *Krapfenwaldl* Waltz. (Several decades later, when Anton Bruckner's students asked him what he had been thinking of when he wrote his seventh symphony, Bruckner thought for a while and said, 'Of the people going to the Krapfenwaldl on Sunday, sitting down and unpacking their Wiener Schnitzel and potato salad.')

In the summer of 1831, the cholera hit Vienna once again. People put up large containers with ashes in their houses and bought yards of 'health flannel' and vinegar. Vinegar-vapours were said to be a sure-fire preventive against the disease, like the ringing of church bells in earlier centuries. Special cholera prayer books were sold, offered with the slogan, 'Trust in God and Our Emperor Franz, and Don't Be Afraid of the Cholera!' People who could afford it left the city and went to Baden where the sulphurous springs would guarantee 'absolute protection'. Johann Strauss, always with it, wrote his waltz *Merry Even in Serious Times*, Opus 48. In spite of the surefire therapies, there were 1,784 dead in Vienna.

In 1834 Strauss wrote the *Gabriele* Waltz which soon became known as the *Totenwalzer* (Death Waltz). Everybody knew that Strauss had been in love with a young countess who had treated him 'without kindness'. She married a young count. Strauss and his band were hired to play for the wedding. Several chroniclers reported that 'the countess collapsed during the first bars of the waltz and died a few minutes later'. Karl Reinöhl, a serious biographer, refuses to believe this story: 'Strauss had too much work in those early years to be able to get seriously involved with women'. But we also know that at that time he *did* get involved, and very seriously.

In April 1836 there was an earthquake in Vienna, followed in May by a total eclipse of the sun. When Herschel, the British astronomer, began his observations of the moon at the Cape of Good Hope, the Viennese newspapers headlined the news, 'Men on the Moon', and published detailed reports of volcanic mountains, deep-blue oceans, and people who had their own language and kept domestic animals. Herschel was said to have seen all this 'and much more'. In the summer a 'scientific' book was published telling about three kinds of living beings on the moon. The 'Selenites' had 'wings, blond hair and flashing eyes'. The 'Vespertiles' looked like 'large bats and they were kept as slaves'. And the 'Beavers' were exactly 'as those on earth'. There was much excitement in Vienna until Herschel returned to England and indignantly revealed the entire swindle.

Johann Strauss cashed in by giving a 'Ball on the Moon' at Dommayer's Casino, on 23 June. A Viennese waltz composer had to be a sort of musical columnist, keeping close to the news and possibly ahead of it. When the opening of the first railroad between Vienna

ABOVE The first train leaving
Vienna, from the title page of
the waltz Strauss wrote for
the occasion.

and Deutsch-Wagram was announced for the autumn of 1837, Strauss
composed the waltz *Eisenbahn-Lust* (Railroad-Joy), Opus 89. Vienna's
coachmen were worried about the new invention that was certain to
ruin them but the Emperor Ferdinand, a kind-hearted though somewhat feeble-minded Habsburg, comforted them, 'Don't worry, this
railroad thing won't last'.

At the time when Lanner and Strauss split up and began performing
'against each other', Vienna had many other attractions. At the
Josefsstadt Theater there was the comedian Wenzel Scholz. The Van
Aken menagerie was a popular success, and the Circus Gymnasticus of
Christoph de Bach was always sold out. But Strauss especially was a
terrific success; nothing could stop him. Within a few years he had an
organization of some two hundred musicians. He would deploy his
musical forces where they were needed. Eduard Hanslick wrote about
these days,

. . . one cannot imagine the wild enthusiasm which the two musicians
created in Vienna . . . innumerable articles appeared about Lanner and
Strauss, enthusiastic, both humorous and serious, and certainly much
longer than those devoted to Mozart and Beethoven. . . . The sweetly in-
toxicating rhythm that took hold of heads and feet eclipsed great and
serious music and made the audience increasingly unfit for any intellectual
effort.

43

In the early nineteenth century the Apollo Hall was the most luxurious establishment in Vienna: five ballrooms, forty-four other public rooms, three glasshouses and thirteen kitchens, 'grottoes and artificial waterfalls, a lake with swans, flowers and trees all winter long'. Contemporary enthusiasts compared the luxury of the Apollo Hall to the splendours of ancient Rome. So were other features of the place: the Apollo was often mentioned in Schranck's *History of Prostitution in Vienna*. It was always easy to find amusing company for a *dolce vita* excursion there. Strauss often performed at the Apollo Hall, and Metternich's police used him and the establishment for its own dark purposes. Metternich said, 'With Strauss and Apollo, you keep the demagogues quiet'.

After Lanner's appointment as *Hofballmusikdirektor* in 1829, Strauss signed a six-year contract with Johann Georg Scherzer, the owner of Sperl's where he had served his apprenticeship under the beer-loving Pamer. Now Strauss returned to Sperl's as the big star. He was just twenty-six. He was not only famous, he already had what we now call charisma.

An announcement of the forthcoming balls to be conducted at Sperl's by the elder Strauss in 1841.

Strauss gave his first concert at Sperl's on 4 October 1829. By that time the fame of the Apollo Hall was declining; a few years later it became a prosaic soap factory. For many years, Sperl's was the artistic home of Strauss. Over a quarter of his new compositions were first performed there. Visitors to Vienna were always told they had to see St Stephen's, the Hofburg, the Capuchin Vault where the Habsburgs were buried, and 'Sperl's and Strauss'. Scherzer, a man of taste, made his establishment the quintessence of Biedermeier elegance; a paradox, actually, since the Biedermeier style was not characterized by grandeur and elegance. At Sperl's there were soft rugs, palm trees, flowers, mirrors, a dining room 'with many hundreds of candles', a winter-garden, and a large park. Many important balls were given there. The Strauss Benefit, on *Fasching* Tuesday, was a famous affair, 'commented on not only in Vienna and Austria'. Later there were imitations of Sperl's in Budapest, Berlin, Madrid, and London. Heinrich Laube (1806–84), the writer who later became a famous director of the Burgtheater, described an evening at Sperl's, in 1833:

The company is quite mixed but the ingredients should not be scorned, and the mixture is classicist-Viennese. An evening and half the night at Sperl's is the key to Vienna's sensuous life, which means Vienna's life. In the middle of the garden there is the orchestra with its seductive siren's sounds, the new waltzes that irritate our learned musicians and excite our young people. In front of the orchestra there stands the modern hero of Austria, *le Napoléon autrichien* – conductor Johann Strauss. What Napoleon's victories meant to the French, the waltzes of Strauss mean to the Viennese, and if they had cannons, they would build Strauss a Vendôme obelisk at Sperl's. The father shows him to his child, the Viennese woman to her foreign lover, the host to his guest. 'That's him!' – 'Who?' – 'He.' As the French say, *voici l'homme*. . . . The man is black as a Moor; his hair is curly; his mouth energetic, his nose snub; if his face were not white he would be the complete king of the Moors. . . . Typically African too is the way he conducts his dances . . . his fiddlebow dances with his arms, the tempo animates his feet. . . . The Viennese accept this passionate procedure with unexampled enthusiasm paying such close attention to their hero and his deeds as it would be well for the German public to pay to some other things.

Laube, the German-born writer, and Hanslick, the critic who came from Prague, both conclude regretfully that the Viennese enthusiasm for the waltz and its composers made them temporarily blind and deaf to the greater genius of Mozart and Beethoven; they might not have thought so if they had been born in Vienna. And Laube concludes, with a sigh of resignation, 'The public greets each waltz rhythm with thunderous cheers. . . . The man tucks his girl deep in his arm, and in a strange way they glide into the rhythm.' The second Johann Strauss wrote much later, 'The years between 1830 and 1836, when my father

Joseph Lanner in his uniform as conductor of the 2nd Vienna City Regiment.

conducted the music at Sperl's, will remain unforgettable in Vienna's musical history.'

Another famous establishment in the waltz-crazy city was the Tivoli in Obermeidling, 'with eighty columns, a truly magnificent view, a large music pavilion, and a chute where on four tracks sixteen small cars were running up and down so fast that one thought one was making a flight through the air. . . . The first such chutes were built in Russia, and the Russians later brought them to Paris and Berlin, and finally to Vienna.' After several weeks of publicity, the Tivoli joined the company of the Apollo Hall, Sperl's, Dommayer's Casino in

Hietzing, and the Water-Glacis. Soon there were Tivoli watches, Tivoli hats, Tivoli 'rockets', and books about the Tivoli. Chopin took a ride on a chute and wrote home, 'It first looked like complete nonsense to me but when we began to slide down I was transformed from a Saulus of this silly Viennese entertainment into a Paulus.' But the Tivoli's glory did not last. Even Strauss could not save the place after 1834. Eventually the Tivoli was sold and became a dairy farm.

For a long time, Joseph Lanner was believed to reflect the cosiness of the Biedermeier; his waltzes were said to reflect the mood of calmness, of naïvety. Today we understand him better. Lanner's modest charm may have helped to create the legend, which was enhanced by his soft, dreamy waltzes. He was at his best playing with his small orchestra under the trees of the Prater. His melodies sounded 'romantic'. He always seemed to court his listeners. The Viennese would say, 'With Lanner, it's "Please, dance, I beg you." With Strauss, "You must dance, I command you."' Strauss was more successful: people always prefer to be commanded than begged.

Today, however, many people feel that Lanner's greatest waltzes are superior to the best written by the older Strauss. Lanner's introduction is often serious, almost solemn, followed by the sudden gaiety of the waltz theme. He is a master of orchestral colours. Lanner can be a true poet, as in the introduction to *The Romanticists*. One feels the affinity with Schubert's ever-present melancholy. 'Lanner's mature waltzes often breathe the fresh air of early romanticism,' writes Mosco Carner, and after a thorough analysis of the waltzes of Lanner and Strauss concludes that 'posterity has given judgement to Lanner'. His finest waltzes are today rated with the best of the younger Johann and Josef. Father Strauss's most famous work is not a waltz but the *Radetzky March*.

The productivity of Lanner and Strauss was astonishing. Both died in their early forties, and each left over 250 works. They *had* to produce new tunes all the time in order to maintain their popularity and income. Waltzes and polkas were hits today and forgotten tomorrow. People always wanted something new. It was a rat race, and contributed to their early death.

Lanner died of typhus on 14 April 1843. He was only forty-two. People were crying, even the *Straussianer* who had been against him. Strauss conducted at his friend's funeral.

3

The 'Scandalous' Waltz

The Viennese Waltz was a nineteenth-century phenomenon. Its era began with Joseph Lanner and ended with the death of the second Johann Strauss in 1899. Its origin is obscure, but its early history is connected with the *ländler* in 3/4 time, the English country dance, and the *Teutsche* (German) dances of Bavaria in the fourteenth century. In the third act of *Die Meistersinger von Nürnberg* the guild apprentices dance a sprightly ländler that has some waltz features. The court conductor Johann Heinrich Schmelzer (1623–80) was one of the first to write three-quarter time dances in Viennese style, preceding Haydn and Schubert.

Around 1750 the new dance called *Walzer* (from *walzen*, the Latin *volvere*, 'to rotate, to roll, to turn') became popular with the peasants in Bavaria, Tyrol and Styria. It was danced by single couples. Gradually the waltz was accepted in the towns where it became more civilized. Attempts to trace the waltz to the French volte or the minuet, both also danced in triple time, were not successful. The somewhat stiff minuet was danced by eighteenth-century upper society while the waltz was a lower class entertainment.

The English country dance came to France late in the seventeenth century, became popular as *contre-danse* and was soon accepted all over the Continent. In Vienna and Germany the upper classes also liked the *Anglaise* and the *Ecossaise* and the French danced the quadrille. While the ladies and gentlemen of the baroque and rococo grew bored with the minuet, the people in the countryside, and later in the suburbs, would embrace one another lustily in three-four time. Word soon got around among the blasé aristocrats that the waltz was a very erotic dance. On the large estates, some noblemen began slipping away to the balls of their servants.

By 1786, the waltz even reached the opera stage, in the second act finale of *Una Cosa Rara*, by the Spanish composer Martín y Soler, which was more successful in Vienna than Mozart's *Le Nozze di Figaro*, performed the same year. Mozart alludes to it ironically when the orchestra plays a few bars from *Una Cosa Rara* during the supper scene in *Don Giovanni*, with Leporello commenting on it approvingly. Mozart's friend, the Irish singer Michael Kelly who sang the stuttering notary Don Curzio in the very first performance of *Figaro* but is now remembered only for his *Reminiscences* (1826), writes about life in Vienna in 1776:

... The people were dancing mad. As the carnival approached, gaiety began to display itself on all sides, and when it really came, nothing could exceed its brilliancy. The ladies of Vienna are particularly celebrated for their grace and movements of waltzing of which they never tire. For my own part, I thought waltzing from ten at night until seven in the morning a continual whirligig, most tiresome to the eye and ear – to say nothing of worse consequences. ...

Kelly's criticism must not be taken too seriously. In his *Reminiscences* he mentions, for instance, a string quartet evening in Mozart's house at which 'the players were tolerable'. They were Joseph Haydn, first violin; the composer Karl Ditters von Dittersdorf, second violin; Mozart, viola; and the composer Jan Baptist Wanhal, cello. Kelly wrote a lot of amusing nonsense but his feelings about the waltz were shared by many people who considered it an immoral dance. The famous dancing master Chavanne pontificated, '*La valse n'a point de rapport avec la bonne dance*'. In 1806, Christian Friedrich Daniel Schubart, in his *Ideas about the Aesthetics of Composition*, called the waltz 'a scandalous dance'.

Such criticism naturally made the waltz very popular with the younger people. By 1815, the waltz had conquered the Congress of Vienna. The unforgotten *bon mot* of the otherwise forgotten Prince de Ligne, 'Le Congrès ne marche pas – il danse', meant exactly that: instead of attention to serious business, the Congress was dancing the waltz. In London Lord Byron attacked the waltz in his poem *The Waltz: an Apostrophic Hymn*, published under the pseudonym of Horace Hornem, Esq. It refers to 'the lewd grasp and lawless contact', and ends, 'And cockneys practise what they can't pronounce'. In 1816 an English dancing master, Thomas Wilson, wrote *A Description of the Correct Method of Waltzing*, in which the waltz was 'generally admitted to be a promoter of vigorous health and productive of an hilarity of spirits . . . certainly not an enemy of true morals'. From its beginning the waltz created controversy and sensation.

The transformation of the robust staccato ländler to the erotic, romantic sweep of the waltz took place in Vienna in the early nineteenth century. Until then the Viennese had been crazy about the *langaus* and the galop. The playwright Adolph Bäuerle (1786–1859), still remembered for his slogan, 'Es gibt nur a Kaiserstadt, 's gibt nur a Wien' ('There's only one imperial city, there's only one Vienna'), wrote:

The Mondschein Hall made an immortal name for itself by the mortality of young people dancing nothing but the *langaus*. It was the fashion to be a daring dancer. The man had to waltz his partner from one end of the hall to the other with the greatest possible speed. . . . The circle had to be made six to eight times at a breathless pace with no pause. Each couple tried to outdo the others, and it was no rare thing for an apoplexy of the lungs to end the madness. Such frightful intermezzi finally caused the police to forbid the *langaus*.

The end of the *langaus* brought the beginning of the waltz as a popular dance among all classes of the population. Three of Kelly's 'tolerable players' – Haydn, Dittersdorf, Mozart – wrote early waltzes. Schubert composed beautiful, slow *ländler* pieces and waltzes that remain the musical echo of the Biedermeier. Later, Schubert's waltzes became more poetic, full of romantic charm. Schubert was among the first to use the basic form: two parts, each part with an eight- or sixteen-bar phrase, repeated, with the first part ending the section. He often achieved strong contrast between a lyrical first and a rhythmical second part; most waltz composers have followed his example. Nevertheless, Schubert's waltzes are for performing rather than dancing, and Lanner and the elder Johann Strauss wrote the first Viennese waltzes that were primarily dances. They extended Schubert's form to include a brief introduction, five sections, each in two parts, and a coda. Both were violinists and wrote their melodies primarily for their instrument. Thus, musically, the Viennese waltz remains closely related to the violin, the Viennese 'house instrument'. For all waltz composers were primarily fiddlers. The great waltz melodies of the second Strauss were conceived in terms of the violin and he thought of his violin mainly as a means of creating and playing waltz melodies. The instrument did not attract him *per se*; he never tried to write solo music for the it.

'A great violinist . . . may cause storms of passions', Schubert wrote in his treatise of composition. He was thinking of Nicolò Paganini. There was a certain affinity between Paganini and the older Strauss, his contemporary, but not so far as actual playing was concerned. Paganini, the greatest violinist of all times, widened the horizons of the instrument and created a new style and technique of violin-playing that has not been surpassed to this day. Johann Strauss was just a dance fiddler and a gifted composer. But both radiated a fascination and sensuous appeal which only a few violinists possess at any time. Both mesmerized their public and exerted an almost hypnotic spell on their audiences.

Some forerunners to the waltz: ABOVE LEFT *La Contredanse*;
BELOW LEFT *La Danse Villageoise*; the stately quadrille (BELOW)
was danced by the upper classes while the common people enjoyed
the robust *ländler* (ABOVE).

The virtuoso violinist Paganini, drawn by Ingres in 1819. His charm and brilliance caused a sensation in Vienna in 1828 and Strauss was quick to write a *Paganini Waltz*, Opus 11.

Paganini sensed this affinity when he attended a Johann Strauss concert in Paris in 1837. Paganini was already suffering from tuberculosis of the larynx, unable to perform in public. He died three years later. He had often struck the imagination and the heart of the Parisians – 'he made them forget death hovering over them while an epidemic of cholera was raging in Paris', Berlioz wrote – and he felt that Strauss – tall, dark, handsome, adored by the women – knew the secret of the old magic. After the concert he walked up to the platform and embraced Johann Strauss, saying, 'I'm delighted to meet you. You've given so much joy to the world.'

The younger Strauss also had the violinist's charisma. Many writers comment on his 'magical' attraction. Women would swoon and men were impressed. It was the phenomenon of mass hypnosis that repeats itself in every generation; in recent times Frank Sinatra did it, and the Beatles. The younger Strauss was also a good pianist, and in later years he often improvised on the harmonium. But as a composer he always had the violin sound in his ear. He spent his early years, as Lanner and his father did before him, standing in front of his orchestra, playing with his men and conducting with his bow, a glorified gypsy primas. His monument in Vienna's Stadtpark, by the sculptor Edmund Hellmer, has caught him in a characteristic pose, standing up, playing.

Carner has described some violinistic features of the Viennese waltz,

... the exploitation of the open strings which explains the frequent choice of G, D, A and E as the main key of the whole waltz set; double-stoppings, euphonious sixths and 'sobbing' thirds which, combined with frequent glissandi, impart to the Viennese waltz a slightly languid, sentimental note; wide leaps over the strings from the E to the G strings; tunes to be played on the fourth string; all the effects produced by different bowing – legato, staccato, spiccato, saltando, sul ponticello, and short, crisp up-bows, notably at the opening of the waltz.

'The secret of the Viennese waltz,' wrote the art critic Hans Tietze, 'is in resolving the oppressive, doubtful elements of the Viennese character into art, in a pure, expressive form.' Throughout the nineteenth century, the waltz remains the very expression of Vienna's 'soul'. Geographically too, the waltz is a child of the Viennese landscape. In musical history this is the exception rather than the rule: the influence of the landscape is often overrated. Mozart, the supergenius, remained independent from his surroundings. He created an artistic universe from his mind, heart and soul. It is difficult to connect the landscape of Saxony with the titanic creations of Johann Sebastian Bach, or the sultry eroticism of *Tristan und Isolde* with the well scrubbed, unerotic atmosphere of Triebschen, overlooking the Lake of Lucerne. It is not difficult to feel the connection between Debussy and Paris, between the lakes and woods of Finland and Sibelius, but Smetana and Dvořák, Bartók and Kodály, Mussorgsky and Borodin expressed the inner voices rather than the landscape of their beloved homelands.

Vienna is a special case. Very few of the composers who there created three great eras in musical history – classicism, romanticism, and modern music, all intimately connected with Vienna – were Viennese. But for centuries Vienna's *genius loci* attracted great composers who came from elsewhere, stayed and wrote music: Gluck from the Palatinate, Haydn from the Hungarian border, Mozart from Salzburg, Beethoven from Bonn, Brahms from Hamburg, Hugo Wolf from Windischgrätz, Bruckner from Upper Austria, Mahler from Bohemia, Richard Strauss from Munich. All of them instinctively felt that music was in the air. In 1762 Mozart's father, sober and down-to-earth, wrote, 'Are all people who come to Vienna bewitched so that they have to stay here? It rather looks like it.'

Vienna's indestructible *joie de vivre* and love of music are old phenomena. In the early nineteenth century, people seeking employment in an aristocratic Viennese palace were expected to play an instrument. Advertisements said, 'Servant wanted who is able to play the violin well and to accompany difficult piano sonatas.'

After the defeat of the Austrian Army against the Prussians at Königgrätz in 1866 many Viennese 'celebrated' by getting drunk. (*Freut euch des Lebens!* [Enjoy life!] is the title of a famous Strauss waltz.) The concerts which Johann Strauss gave in the weeks following the lost war were always crowded. The poet L. A. Frankl was very angry when he saw two thousand people at a Venetian Summer Ball at the Prater. The Viennese remained incorrigible optimists. So did Johann Strauss who wrote *The Blue Danube* the following year. Had he been a pessimist, he might never have created what Decsey called 'the very sound of Austria'.

Vienna's astonishing ability to live with, and survive, disaster attracted people from everywhere. And it was the mixture-as-never-before which, in turn, created the special mood of the city, filled with merriment and music. Vienna's geographical location and its imperishable charm bewitched people, as Leopold Mozart had noticed. Even the conquerors became conquered by the *genius loci*. It was no secret after the last war that the Soviet occupation forces had to be rotated quickly because their morale was badly shaken by the frivolous atmosphere of the Danube capital.

The great Viennese waltzes are the quintessence of the *genius loci*. Johann Strauss's finest waltzes contain Slav, Hungarian, Bavarian, Italian, even French elements but they are perfectly blended and what emerges is *der Wiener Walzer*, the Viennese waltz that has never been successfully imitated.

There were three types of the waltz in Vienna. The oldest was a slow version of the ländler, with three equal crotchets. Lanner and Johann Strauss changed this rhythm into a minim followed by a crotchet, which gave many of their melodies a soft, sensuous lilt. The second Johann Strauss developed and refined this rhythm and created the *Verzückungswalzer* (bewitching waltz) that made people delirious, with its daring harmonies and ever-changing rhythms. They remain both timeless and modern. A whole evening of the dances of Father Strauss might be somewhat monotonous, but two hours of the waltzes, polkas and marches of his son are an unmitigated delight.

Musicians love this music, too. Some of the greatest have loved it best. They were able to hear, earlier than ordinary people, the inner tension and hidden beauty of the great waltzes. When Strauss heard *Parsifal* in Bayreuth in 1892, he was amused by, and pleased with, the seductive Flower Maiden's scene, an erotic waltz theme. He may have thought of himself, and he was right. Wagner had learned the secret of the seduction waltz from Strauss. It cannot be analysed; its elements are an unfathomable mixture of melody, rhythm, harmony, joy and sadness, nostalgia and vitality, and happiness in spite of everything. As a dance it is demanding. If it is well done, it gives the dancers no chance of conversation. Yet this silent dance is also the most sensuous. Perhaps this is the reason that it has survived taste and fashion, currents and fads in an age of unreason that places feeling above intellect.

Music and civilization remain closely connected. The 'Old Vienna' of Schubert, Lanner and the elder Strauss was the Gothic city (today known as First District) surrounded by ramparts, suburbs and the vineyards and villages of the Vienna Woods. The earlier waltzes reflect the cosy atmosphere of the parochial town, when there was time for reflection and meditation. By contrast, the great waltzes of the second Strauss, those written after 1860, mirror the hectic gaiety and nervous tension of the latter part of the century, when Vienna became for a short time the glittering Imperial city, the sophisticated capital of Europe. Within one generation the Strauss dynasty graduated from the wine gardens of the suburbs to the pompous elegant ballrooms of the city. From there the younger Strauss made the steep climb to the gold stucco and the immortality of Grosser Musikvereinsaal where the symphonies of Brahms, Bruckner and Mahler were performed for the first time – and his own great waltzes.

Although he was too modest to say so, Strauss in his late days thought of his best waltzes as symphonic music. They might still be played for dancing, but he hoped that people would one day listen to

OPPOSITE A cartoon entitled 'Viennese waltzes'.

der Volkskinder Walzer

der pädagogische Walzer

der Entscheidungswalzer

der "höchste" Walzer

Hofball-Walzer

der Jubiläumswalzer

Pechvogels erster und letzter Walzer

W. Grögler

them in the concert hall. His wish has been fulfilled: in Austria, Germany and other countries great orchestras under celebrated conductors perform his music.

At his fiftieth jubilee in 1894 Strauss, in a short, embarrassed speech, described his waltzes as 'my feeble attempts to extend the form handed down to me by my father and Joseph Lanner'. He was honest and much too modest. He not only extended the waltz form, he gave it a new dimension. In his early waltzes the introduction is often as short as in those of his father, but later he turns them into orchestra preludes. In *Wein, Weib und Gesang* the introduction is seventeen pages of orchestral score, in the *Emperor Waltz* ten pages. In the introduction to *The Blue Danube* the tremolo strings create the glistening, dancing lights playing on the waves of the river. Strauss did not attempt musical description: he wanted to convey impressions. He had taken his cue from the title page of the *Pastoral* Symphony: 'more an expression of feeling than painting'. The symphonic style of his introductions does not make symphonies out of his waltzes. They lead into the waltz themes, which often open quietly, reach a climax and subside again.

The unique introductions are matched by some unique codas: nineteen pages of the score in *The Blue Danube*, twenty-two in the *Emperor Waltz*. The mood is nostalgic, a short, last reminiscence; there is a moment of sadness – life goes so fast, and with it everything that is beautiful – but in the very end there is that final expression of live-and-let-live.

However, it is the waltz itself, regardless of the beauty of introduction and coda, that makes the dance music. The younger Strauss began with themes of conventional eight-, twelve- or sixteen-bar length; even when there seems to be an extra bar, it turns out to be the up-beat or the end of an uneven rhythm. Later he extended his melodic span. *Aus den Bergen (From the Mountains)*, Opus. 292, has a theme of almost ninety bars. Ironically he dedicated this waltz to Eduard Hanslick who had earlier accused Strauss of writing a 'waltz requiem' in the *Sound Waves Waltz*.

The younger Strauss combined Lanner's poetic charm with his father's élan and rhythm; thus he created the waltz that had everything. He kept the basic form, but he gave it enormous scope with his depth of feeling, sweep of melody and wealth of instrumentation. His moods range from the sensuous and sentimental to the humorous and capricious. Sometimes he breaks up the one-two-three of a melody with a one-two pattern in the accompaniment, creating contrast.

'Strauss is an artist,' wrote Berlioz after his second visit to Vienna. 'One doesn't appreciate enough the influence which he exercised on musical feeling in Europe by introducing the interplay of various

OPPOSITE A lithograph by Albrecht showing various scenes of entertainment during the carnival season.

The Danube river flowing through the village of Nussdorf, near Vienna, in the early nineteenth century. The spire of St Stephens can be seen through the trees.

rhythms into his waltzes. The effect is so stimulating that the dancers subconsciously dance a two-step waltz, though the music keeps in 3/4 time.' And he compared 'the veritable art' of the Viennese waltz with 'the routine of our Parisian balls'. Strauss knew some dancers might get irritated, but he didn't care; he wanted to write beautiful music. He was confident he could break the rules and get away with it.

Gluck and Haydn, Mozart and Beethoven personally rehearsed their new compositions with the orchestra in Vienna. They would explain to the musicians exactly how they wanted the music to be played. There was no need to put every crescendo or ritardando in the score. The waltz composers followed the local tradition. It is not known exactly how Lanner and the members of the Strauss family performed their works. Many of the original scores are lost. Yet somehow a tradition of how the music should be played has survived in Vienna. It is generally agreed that the great waltzes must not be played too fast. Strauss occasionally reminded his brother Eduard of this.

The metronome speed for a full bar varies between 60 and 70. The waltzes of the first Strauss are often played a little faster than those of his sons, Johann and Josef. (Eduard's compositions are not very important.) Today many interpreters of Strauss's music go back to the traditions established by Wilhelm Wacek who played in the orchestra of Eduard Strauss until 1901 when it was dissolved.

The Viennese custom is slightly to anticipate the second beat, conveying a faster, lighter rhythm. There is often also a slight ritardando at the opening of the waltz theme, 'gliding into' the true tempo. There are breaks of the phrase which, the Viennese claim, only a born-and-bred Viennese can do properly because 'it's all a matter of feeling'. Either you have it, or you don't – in which case no one can help you.

The concert waltzes of the younger Strauss evoke a wide range of feelings – bittersweet memories of love and youth, briefly recaptured, a touch of let's-be-merry-for-tomorrow-we-die. Their inner vibrations touch the heart and affect soul and mind. No one as yet checked the collective blood pressure of the audience at the New Year's Eve concert of the Vienna Philharmonic (repeated in the morning of New Year's Day) when Willi Boskovsky lifts his violin and bow, the way Johann Strauss did, for the introduction to *The Blue Danube*. A long-suppressed sigh is heard, followed by applause. At last! Everybody has been waiting for it. Then the music begins once more; many people smile happily. Few pieces of music have such a universal effect. The concert is televised all over the world; last year's estimated audience was five hundred million people. All year long Boskovsky receives grateful letters from all over the world. So many millions of people cannot be wrong.

No one has surpassed Johann Strauss as a waltz composer. Even Franz Lehàr's best waltzes – the best since Strauss – lack his depth and vitality, his spontaneity and exhilaration. Felix Mottl, a famous conductor, wrote in 1894, 'As a born Viennese, I recognize in Johann Strauss's musical language my own native tongue. I prefer a great Strauss waltz to the learned, carefully done works of our modern classics because I consider music an emotional art that must not be diluted by unnecessary calculation and mathematics. The musical world has been poor in ideas since the death of Wagner. Strauss is the exception: he still has ideas, a master touched by genius.'

4
The Austrian Napoleon

On 14 March 1825 Johann Strauss, 'without parents, *Musikus*, un-married' applied for a passport to Graz, Styria, 'to earn money'. Three weeks later his guardian Anton Müller, '*bürgerlicher* clothesmaker', asked the local council to permit Strauss to marry Anna Streim 'before be sets out on his journey'. The ceremony took place on 11 July, in Liechtental parish church. The bride's father, a former coachman, was the proprietor of a popular inn, The Red Cock, in the suburb of Liech-tental. Herr Josef Streim had made the difficult climb from servant to the bourgeois, and was not overjoyed that his daughter was marrying a musician. There was nothing he could do: Anna was expecting a baby.

They had met at the inn where Strauss had been performing with Lanner's orchestra, shortly before the two friends split up. A family legend claims that Anna's mother was descended from a Spanish grandee. Actually her family, Rober (or Robert), had come to Vienna from Luxemburg which was then part of the Austrian Netherlands. At the wedding Anna was twenty-four, her husband three years younger. An early picture shows an attractive woman, her dark hair piled up high *à la chinoise*, with a proud bearing and a natural dignity: a woman able to cope with every situation among all classes; certainly not the housewife type.

Their first child, Johann, was born on 25 October. In the baptismal register the twenty-one-year-old father signed his profession as music teacher. After breaking with Lanner on 1 September, he had begun teaching the violin and the piano. Not for long though. During the *Fasching* of 1826 he was already conducting his own orchestra of fourteen men. The first waltz, later published under his name, was the *Täuberl Waltz*, after the Two Doves Inn for which he wrote it. His first real success was the *Kettenbrücken Waltz*, also called after an inn where he often performed. Three years later Johann Strauss was already the

Latecomers running to a Strauss ball at Die Goldene Birne.

most famous waltz composer in Vienna. 'The Kaiserstadt [Vienna] never had so many men writing waltzes at any previous time', writes Fritz Lange. Strauss sensed that his public wanted glamorous excitement rather than the serene pleasures that people got from Lanner. Otto Rommel, the theatre historian and literary editor, calls the violence in Strauss's music and its influence on the audiences 'the outstanding, if not the only characteristic of Vienna's *Vormärz* culture'. 'Pre-March' was the era preceding the Revolution of March 1848, when intellectuals, students and workers got increasingly restless, and Metternich's police reacted with increasing brutality. Strauss's timing was right. He felt that an era was coming to an end, even though he was not sure what would come next.

Within ten years of his marriage there were six children. After Johann, the eldest, Josef was born in 1827, Anna in 1829, Therese in 1831, Ferdinand in 1834 (he died in infancy), and Eduard in 1835. Yet family life did not make him settle down, and if Johann Strauss was the 'Napoleon of the dance' when he performed with his orchestra, at home he was a difficult husband and impossible father, moody and restless. The marriage was already on the rocks; the magic had gone out of it, and he was no longer interested in his wife or his children.

He was a complex man of many contradictions. He was happy and exuberant only as the public figure, but afterwards he often suffered from melancholy that he may have inherited from his father, who had committed suicide. He was a difficult employer. Once he almost fired a musician for missing a cue in a Beethoven overture, but he did not hesitate to hire a male imitator of women's voices who had a great success with Rosina's cavatina, *Una voce poco fà* from *Il Barbiere di Siviglia*. His concerts were often accompanied by fireworks.

Soon Vienna became too small for him: his restless nature drove him further afield. After earlier trips to Hungary and Germany he made a long German tour in 1835, went to North Germany, Holland, Belgium, the Rhineland the following year; and to Belgium, France and England in 1837. That tour lasted over a year, at the end of which Strauss suffered the breakdown from which he never completely recovered.

He arrived in Paris with his orchestra late in October 1837, at the right moment. Heine had written a successful book, *De l'Allemagne*, in 1835, and Madame de Staël had started what soon became a pro-

A large cart carries guests to a Strauss ball.

German vogue. Victor Hugo, Gérard de Merval, Théophile Gautier wrote about Germany. At the first Strauss concert on 1 November all great composers living in Paris were present: Adam, Auber, Berlioz, Halévy, Cherubini, Meyerbeer. The clarinettist Reichmann, a member of the orchestra, wrote to friends in Vienna, 'We've won a victory. And what did the battle cost which our *Meister* directed with his baton? A few horsehairs, rosin for one sou, and a few deep breaths.' After the second concert, at the Tuileries, the *Journal des Débats* wrote, 'Les valses de Strauss obtiennent une immense succès.'

A few days later, Strauss performed for Louis Philippe, the Citizen-King, and his guest Leopold, King of the Belgians. Less than nine years after Strauss had joined Lanner's band in the Prater of Vienna, Strauss had become *hoffähig* – worthy to be received at the court. After the concert the King pressed his hands and thanked him 'for giving me the honour of your performance'. The Duke of Orléans took his violin and tried to play it, and the Queens of France and Belgium joined Strauss while champagne was being offered. The next morning, the King sent him 2000 francs and a diamond pin. In the *Journal des Débats* the brilliant, incorruptible music critic Hector Berlioz admired 'the fire, the intelligence and the poignant rhythmic coquetry' of Johann Strauss and his orchestra.

A Parisian musical evening in the reign of Louis Philippe.

After Strauss's success the two important Paris conductors, Alfred Musard and Jean Dufresne, had tried to start a first-class intrigue against *le Napoléon autrichien*, but instead of fighting his competitors Strauss joined forces with Musard. They would jointly give thirty concerts. Strauss and his men would play before intermission, Musard and his orchestra of two hundred afterward. Most of the critics preferred the chamber-orchestral forces of the Strauss ensemble. Berlioz wrote about 'the twenty-six artists that Strauss brought from Vienna. Four first violins and four second ones, two cellos, two double basses, two flutes, two clarinets, one bassoon, one oboe, two trumpets, two horns, one trombone, one kettledrum, one big drum, and one harp. But since most of the artists own several instruments and change them very quickly, the Strauss orchestra switches light and shadow, and seems twice as big.'

On 23 December there was the first mutiny among the musicians, who were getting homesick and wanted to return to Vienna. They did not like Christmas in Paris, where the people had no trees and celebrated by staying up all night, drinking and dancing. Strauss promised his men more money, and said they were staying in Paris for the carnival. Between 27 December and 28 February of the following year the orchestra performed every night, either concerts or at private balls. At the Austrian Embassy there were ovations for Strauss. Anastasius Grün, the poet whom Metternich did not like, made a wonderful speech about Strauss. Strauss looked pale and thin. It was said that he had not had a proper night's rest in weeks.

He could not have coped without his closest friend, Carl Friedrich Hirsch, who had come along as a sort of manager. As a boy, Hirsch had studied harmony for a year with Beethoven, but the experience was not encouraging: Beethoven had no patience with his less gifted pupils. Hirsch became an official at the War Bookkeeping Agency – something many countries should have now. Later he became confidential and financial adviser to the first Strauss who earned a lot of money but always managed to spend more than he earned.

When Strauss was away on his long tours, it never occurred to him that his wife in Vienna, with six children to look after, needed money. Fortunately Hirsch took care of it. His hobbies were lamps, lights and fireworks. He was a precursor of today's lighting technicians who have created a science, lighting up highways and buildings, airports and theatre stages. Hirsch would light up the Johann Strauss concerts at Augarten, putting up lights and lamps. People called him the Lamperl-Hirsch.

He helped Strauss to quell the serious mutiny that broke out when the musicians were told they were not going home but to London. They had been away from their families for several months.

Champagne was all right, but a glass of cheap *Heuriger* in a lovely garden around Vienna was better. Somehow Strauss and Hirsch got the orchestra to England. They landed in Dover on 11 April 1838 after a rough Channel crossing.

Everything went wrong in England. The hotel was bad and the food was worse. Prince Paul Anton Esterházy, the Austrian ambassador, warned Strauss 'to avoid all excesses', to read his contracts carefully, and keep all cash in the bank, not in the hotel room. Unfortunately Strauss ignored Esterházy's advice, and money was stolen. Strauss found himself in debt, and was hauled into court. An English music publisher, a certain Cocks, came to his rescue. In return Strauss had to write him a waltz. Despite an exclusive contract with Tobias Haslinger in Vienna he wrote the amusing *Bastille Waltz* (with a faint suggestion of prison), and later explained to Haslinger that it had been *force majeur*.

Afterwards the situation improved. On 18 April *The Times* wrote of a Strauss concert in the Hanover Square Rooms:

> The pieces performed were chiefly his own waltzes, but they are done in a manner most extraordinary and altogether novel in this country. . . . The most eccentric instruments such as bells, castanets, cracking whips etc. are occasionally introduced, and the construction of many pieces is highly fantastic yet never is the precision lost for an instant.

Carl Hirsch, a close friend of the elder Strauss, was responsible for beautiful illuminations at the concerts.

The advertisement for a Strauss
concert in Hanover Square.

OPPOSITE A music cover from
c. 1840 showing Albert and
Victoria dancing.

The paper said that 'from the immense fame which Herr Strauss had
acquired in Vienna a more numerous audience might have been
expected', but attributed this to the lack of publicity. Ignaz
Moscheles, the piano virtuoso, wrote about the impression Strauss
made on the English public, 'He's dancing *corps et âme* while he plays,
not with his feet but with his fiddle that goes up and down while he
beats time with his body.' The *Morning Post* wrote:

So perfect a band was never heard before on this side of the Channel. The
accuracy, the sharpness, the exquisite precision with which every passage
is performed can be the result only of the most careful and persevering
practice . . . Strauss imparts much of his own spirit to the land, the combined effect of which resembles the unity of one single, powerful element.

Seventy years before Mahler and Toscanini preached the artistic
principle of precision and faithful interpretation, the elder Strauss had
strict ideas about performance. Nothing is known about his rehearsal
methods, but we know that he was severe with his musicians. They
were not permitted to mingle with the audience during intervals
or even to dance, as members of M. Musard's orchestra had done in
Paris. Strauss also forbade alcohol on performance days. He himself
never drank. Such was the orchestra's precision that one London critic
wondered 'whether Arnold & Dent send their chronometers hither
[instead of to Greenwich] to ascertain whether they keep true Strauss
time'.

The *Musical World* called Strauss 'the Crœsus of waltz composers,
the modern Midas . . . who evinces great tact and considerable
originality', and continued,

His strength lies in an ingenuity of detail, a striking brilliancy, strong
colouring, and extreme contrasts. . . . In his melodies he displays much
clearness of design and great boldness of outline. The performance of his
music is most remarkable for precision and unanimity of sentiment . . .

The critics in England (which some arrogant German critics called
das Land ohne Musik) had well understood the art of Johann Strauss.
During the coronation of Queen Victoria (28 June) the Strauss
orchestra, standing in front of the Reform Club, played *God save the
Queen* in the middle of a chaotic noise of ringing bells, booming
cannons, shouting people, and the sounds of other bands also playing
the hymn. Prior to the coronation there had been three weeks of
concerts, balls and garden parties. Often the Strauss orchestra would
perform three times a day. There might be a matinee in an aristocratic
house, an afternoon concert at a castle and an evening performance
in London.

The Austrian ambassador gave a ball and appeared arm in arm with
Prince Schwarzenberg and Strauss. At the Duke of Sutherland's ball

68

La Valse à deux temps.

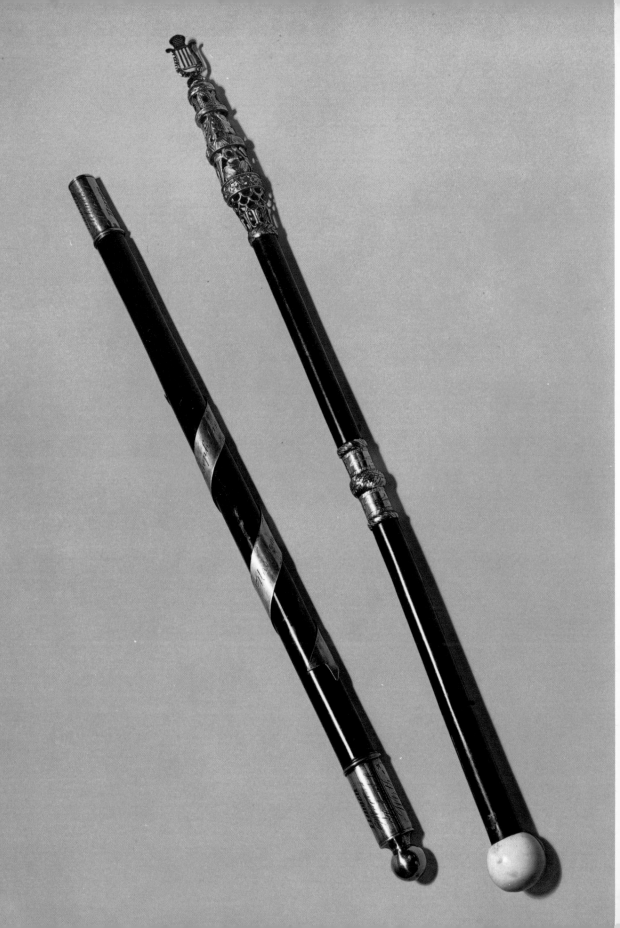

An English lithograph of *c.* 1850 showing a couple dancing the waltz.

Strauss was 'accepted as guest, not musician'. The Baroness Rothschild had a small hall built on her estate for a Strauss concert. After the first State ball in Buckingham Palace, the *Court Gazette* reported that 'a temporary stage for Strauss's Waltz Band was put up on the southern side of the ballroom. . . . The Band performed Strauss's entire new set of waltzes entitled *Hommage à la Reine d'Angleterre*, which were much admired by Her Majesty.' (In 1885, Eduard Strauss, Johann's youngest son, came with his orchestra to London. Queen Victoria, well remembering how his father had played for her, permitted herself a brief moment of nostalgia.)

Having given eighty-six concerts in Paris, Strauss and his men now gave seventy-two concerts in England in 120 days. Strauss would get as much as £200 for a night. In Vienna the *Theaterzeitung* reported that Strauss made 'at least 50,000 guilders during the coronation, that men everywhere smoked Strauss pipes, and women drank tea from Strauss cups'.

North and south, east and west, they went all over England. Birmingham, Liverpool, Reading, Cheltenham, Worcester, Leicester,

OPPOSITE Lanner's baton (TOP) is of black polished wood with a silver band; the ebony baton with the ivory globe belonged to the elder Strauss.

ECHOES OF THE PALACE BALL ROOM.

A CHOICE SELECTION OF THE · COMPOSED EXPRESSLY BY · QUADRILLES · WALTZES, GALOPS &c

MUSARD, STRAUSS, LANNER, LABITSKI, &c

AND ARRANGED FOR THE

PIANO FORTE,

BY

T. VALENTINE & S. J. RIMBAULT.

Ent. Sta. Hall.

Nº

LONDON, D'ALMAINE & Cº SOHO SQUARE

Derby, Nottingham, Sheffield, Leamington, Bath, Southampton, Brighton, Portsmouth. Sometimes the musicians did not see a room for two or three days, trying to catch a few hours' sleep in the mail coach which took them from one place to the next. Strauss was pale and restless, as if in a trance. In Dublin he suggested to the musicians that they go to America, 'You will all get rich there.' They turned him down. So they went south again, to France. One night in Rouen a concert had to be interrupted. The musicians refused to go on: they demanded to return home immediately. One member of the orchestra said it was an open secret that Strauss had no intention of ever going back to his family in Vienna. That was the reason he wanted to take them to America.

Strauss did not answer. He was deeply hurt. For weeks he did not speak a private word to his musicians. There was a new wave of rebellion in early October in Halifax. They had had enough of the English climate, English food and the crazy rat race. In early November they were on their way to Edinburgh. It had been raining for ten days, the roads were flooded, and the coaches were filled with pools of water. When they reached Edinburgh at last, they were all sick. An old Scottish doctor prescribed plenty of hot red wine, nutmeg and ginger, 'enough to wake up the dead'. Most of the musicians recovered, but Strauss remained feverish and was coughing, as they played in Glasgow, Newcastle, Leeds and Derby. The doctor gave him opium against the cough. Strauss fainted several times. He realized at last they could not go on.

They crossed the Channel on the way to France, and gave another concert in Calais. During the third waltz Strauss collapsed on the platform and had to be carried out. He was taken to Paris where he arrived on 9 December. The doctors said he was very ill, and needed at least one month of complete rest. Strauss did not want to go back to Vienna as a sick man, but he had to go: the musicians were already on their way and would tell there what had happened.

In Strasbourg he had another collapse and was taken to a hotel with a 'nervous fever'. For four days he was unconscious. London's *Musical World* which had called Strauss several months ago 'the Crœsus of waltz composers' now thought it was 'a good time for the inculcation of a little morality . . . by a word of advice to those who are disposed to make money too fast, and damage their constitutions, their fame and worst of all – music itself, by a horrid greediness after the receipts of concerts. "Be warned in time, ye itinerant speculators," observe what we shall say of the fate of Strauss, and tremble.'

After reporting, gleefully, that Strauss was 'much applauded, rich – and dying', the paper admitted, 'Since writing we have not heard any fatal news of Strauss. If by any chance he should recover – we shall not permit such an accident to spoil the *moral* of our biography – and enter our protest accordingly.'

In Strasbourg several doctors warned Strauss that he might not survive the long journey to Vienna. He shook his head. Now he wanted to go there. If he had to die he would die in Vienna, he said to Reichmann who had remained with him. At Linz he had another relapse, and ran from his hotel room in a delirium into the cold street where he collapsed. The nightmarish journey almost ended fatally. Near Vienna the horses bolted, and were only just restrained from overturning the coach.

Several friends were waiting for Strauss in Purkersdorf, the last mail station before Vienna. He had forbidden that his wife be notified. When they arrived at the Hirschenhaus, she was said to be at the theatre. Somebody went for her, and he was carried up to his room. When she arrived, neighbours informed her with characteristic cheerfulness that her husband was going to die. It was only a matter of hours. People in Vienna are fond of disaster as long as it does not concern them personally. The boys stood around the father's bed: Johann, thirteen; Josef, eleven; Eduard, three.

Strauss did not die, however, but he never quite recovered from his breakdown. And he had learned nothing. As soon as the doctors permitted him to get up, he reorganized his orchestra and signed some new contracts.

He was very famous now. The Viennese admire their own people, especially after they have been discovered abroad. Strauss made his first appearance after his sickness at Sperl's on 13 January 1839. He was received by ten minutes of applause and ovations. He had come back; now people felt how much they had missed him. True, they had Lanner, but 'Strauss is Strauss'. Everybody had been talking about him, 'even in the poor people's kitchens where some ate a watery soup to save a few *kreuzer* so that they could buy a ticket at Sperl's that night'. Strauss had written a new waltz for the occasion. He called it *Freuden Grüsse (Joy and Greetings)*. It even had a motto: 'Everywhere good, at home the best!' In June 1839 he composed the *London Season Waltz*. It was first performed at Sperl's during a flower festival. On 11 February 1840 he premiered *The Myrtle Waltz*. It was inscribed 'for the wedding of Her Majesty Queen Victoria to His Royal Highness Prince Albert of Saxe-Coburg'.

Despite his fame and popularity Strauss had his setbacks. The musical academy had been conducted by Lanner for the coronation of Emperor Ferdinand as King of Lombardy in Milan in 1838. After Lanner's dismissal as *Hofballmusikdirektor* the position was not given to Strauss but to Philipp Fahrbach, a member of his own orchestra. The powerful court bureaucrats had not forgotten that

The Myrtle Waltz, written for the wedding of Victoria and Albert.

Strauss had been away too long from Vienna.

In Paris Strauss had seen and studied a new dance, the French quadrille. On 5 May 1840 he introduced at the Volksgarten the *Viennese Carnival Quadrille,* Opus 124. He wrote several potpourris. The potpourri (or *quodlibet*) was a mixture of musical scenes from operas, farces, singspiels, songs and couplets that had become very popular. A potpourri was easy to enjoy, with no intellectual effort on the part of the listeners 'many of whom were tired of the cultural demands of life in the elegant salons'. (The second Strauss later included thirty of his father's potpourris in the Complete Edition.)

Strauss was still working too hard. He had another collapse, and the doctors talked of a kidney ailment. At the Hirschenhaus he had moved out of the family apartment into a couple of rooms where he was not bothered by the noise of the children. They made him nervous, and he was particularly upset about the eldest boy, Johann, who was mad about music. He had frequent fights with his wife about the children. Anna had lent the boy one of her husband's violins. His friends told the father that Johann and Josef were good pianists. He had forgotten his own problems when he was a boy, and he did not like his wife to take the side of his sons. He may have meant well. His boys 'should have it better'. He had learned the ups and downs of the musician's profession, and he wanted his boys to have a secure, bourgeois life where everything was well ordered, from promotion to pension. Anna said that he himself had shown the boys the glamour and the excitement of his career. He was unwilling to admit it, and there was

ABOVE A *Zeiselwagen* taking
the Viennese to a ball outside
the centre.

BELOW Couples arriving at
Sperl's in 1840. Over a quarter
of Strauss's new compositions
were first performed there.

another fight. Johann Strauss was a *charmeur* at Sperl's but at home he was a dictator and house tyrant.

People in Vienna suspected that he must be a very rich man, and the newspapers wrote about the 'enormous sums of money' he earned. The reports were not always exaggerated, but the papers did not say how much he spent. On tours he insisted on good hotels and the best food for the members of his orchestra. He knew that this was one way of keeping them satisfied. In Paris, Strauss had paid over 300 francs (gold francs) every day for the rooms occupied by his men. An average day in England cost £100, over 1000 guilders. 'Strauss', a musician wrote to Vienna, 'always puts us up at the best hotels, and orders so many dishes at the best *table d'hôte* that we don't know whether to eat or drink them. Rich travellers couldn't lead a more luxurious life.'

Even in Vienna the expenses were very high. At a summer concert in the Brühl, a suburban resort, Hirsch, his financial adviser and cashier, took in 2800 guilders – certainly a great deal of money. But the expenses amounted to 2500 guilders: lighting (700 guilders), installation of the platform and the tribunes, police, payment to the musicians and advertising (over 100 guilders). After an exhausting evening Strauss kept less than 300 guilders.

First there had been gossip, and then everybody in Vienna was talking about it: Strauss was in love with another woman. He had met Emilie Trambusch some time in 1833. Many Viennese women who adored Strauss said Emilie was 'just a milliner'. Yes, the men said, but *very* attractive. One biographer describes her 'pretty face, vivacious eyes, her way of moving her hips when she walked'. A very sexy woman, and Strauss was 'obsessed by her'. The women said that Emilie wanted expensive clothes and jewellery. The men said that Strauss was an artist, 'and an artist is not bound by conventions'. Victorian prudery was never at home in Catholic Vienna where anything went, and not only during the *Fasching*. 'The men of the *Vormärz* [Pre-March] lived in a sort of fever and rebellion', writes Decsey and he quotes Johann Strauss and Ferdinand Raimund.

Strauss had no political problems but many personal ones. His sixth child, Eduard, had been born early in 1835. Two months later, in May, he had his first child, a girl, from Emilie. By 1844 he had had six other children by her. Two boys lived only a few weeks. During these years when his private life was hectic, to say the least, he wrote some of his best music. On 19 August 1843 he first performed the *Loreley-Rhein-Klänge* at the Water-Glacis, his finest waltz, 'a romantic experience in waltz time which leaves a mystical feeling of longing', (Decsey).

In 1844 Anna Strauss sued for divorce. It was a bitter fight, and at one time Anna had Strauss's band uniforms seized when he refused to support her. They were divorced in 1846, and Strauss moved out of the Hirschenhaus and lived at Lilienbrunngasse 18. The following year he made a will in favour of Emilie and her children and moved with them into Kumpfgasse 11 in the old part of the town.

Strauss and Emilie called their eldest son Johann which was perhaps not in good taste since he had already a son called Johann from his wife. Not much is now known of the children he had by Emilie. One girl became an actress. Another sold artificial flowers. The younger Johann Strauss never talked about them, but it was no secret that he supported them. After the death of Father Strauss Emilie lived in poverty. She did not mourn for long, however: in 1850 she had a daughter by somebody else in Vienna.

The last years of the first Strauss were beset by financial problems. He earned much, but not enough to support two households and so many children. There was never enough money. He had informed Anna through his lawyer that he would not support his sons if they studied music. Without Hirsch, who secretly gave money to Anna, things might have been very bad. Strauss himself was as restless as ever. In 1844 he took his orchestra to Moravia, Bohemia, Dresden, Magdeburg, Berlin. At Kroll's Garden he gave a special performance for the Crown Prince of Prussia (later Emperor Wilhelm 1) who came with princes, generals and members of Berlin's society. In 1845 Strauss was named *Hofballmusikdirektor*. It was said that the court bureaucrats 'couldn't afford to overlook him any longer'. The appointment came too late, however, to give Strauss any real satisfaction. He was no longer *the* Johann Strauss in Vienna. His eldest son had become his competitor.

5
Debut at Nineteen

Johann Strauss the younger – today *the* Johann Strauss – was born on 25 October 1825, under the sign of Scorpio, in a modest two-storey house in Rofranogasse 15, in the St Ulrich (now Neubau) district.

Today the address would be Lerchenfelder Strasse 15. The house was called Zur goldenen Eule (The Golden Owl). Strauss often walked there in his late years, all by himself, and looked at it, as we all look back, with wonderment and regret. He was then rich and famous and lived in a palace. He had come a long way from the unpretentious *Bürgerhaus*, and remained nostalgic for it. In 1825, his mother had been twenty-four and his father twenty-one. The son understood that the beginning of the tragedy had been there, right from the beginning of their marriage.

He hardly remembered his father in those early years; he had always been away, playing somewhere in Vienna, or travelling abroad. Anna had given much warmth and time to her husband, and after she had lost him, she gave her affection to the younger Johann. He was her favourite child. Their relationship remained close until she died.

Anna Strauss had strong convictions. Once she had the courage to attend a Lanner concert and to stand up for her husband's friend. When she became convinced that Johann and his younger brother Josef were gifted musicians, she helped them, risking her husband's wrath. 'My father was a musician by the grace of God,' the son later wrote deferentially about his father. 'If his innermost impulse had not been irresistible, the difficulties that opposed him in his younger years might have pushed him into a different *métier*.' In later years he always tried to understand the father, and never wrote a reproachful word about him.

Little is known about the family's private life in the Hirschenhaus (today Taborstrasse 17). There was always the sound of music. There were his father's instruments. When Father Strauss had his own rooms

The younger Johann Strauss in
1843, the year before he first
came to rival his father's
popularity.

His grandmother's house at
Salmannsdorf, where at the age
of six Johann wrote his first
waltz tune.

Anna Strauss, the mother of
young Johann, who encouraged
him to learn music despite his
father's disapproval.

away from the family apartment, there were often men there rehearsing his latest pieces. Strauss himself was a despot, but fascinating – a glamorous dictator. As far as the boy could think back he had wanted to be like his father. While Strauss tried to keep music away from his boys, they were thinking only of music.

The family would spend the summers in a small house in Salmannsdorf that belonged to their maternal grandmother. Salmannsdorf, still a lovely suburb, has kept a trace of Biedermeier cosiness. There the six-year-old Johann practised on a small table piano and composed a waltz tune, simple and melodious. His mother wrote it down and called it *Erster Gedanke (First Thought)*.

The family grew, and moved twice before they stayed at the Hirschenhaus, a communal apartment house with seventy-seven tenants, four storeys high. The large courtyard was the children's playground. Johann remembered the barrel-organ men who came playing 'Father's waltzes'. The Danube and the Danube Canal were not far away. In the spring when the ice broke there were often floods, and the people had to walk on hastily laid boards.

In his Preface to his father's Collected Works Strauss says nothing about life at the Hirschenhaus. Eduard in his *Memoirs* denies expressly that there were 'dissonances'. The denial itself is significant. The father had strict ideas about the education of his two elder boys: Johann was to become a merchant or a banker, Josef an architect and engineer. Solid bourgeois professions. And they would study languages. On his travels he often regretted that he had never learned French and English as a boy. He even tolerated the boys' piano lessons; in every family in Vienna the children were supposed 'to learn to play an instrument'. But not professionally. He listened to the boys only after Tobias Haslinger had told him how well they played piano duets.

He did not know that Johann yearned to play the violin, and that the boy was secretly taking lessons from Franz Amon, his father's first violinist. Anna Strauss, of course, was in on the conspiracy. To pay for his violin lessons Johann gave piano lessons to the son of a tailor and to a thirteen-year-old girl, both living in the house. He got 60 kreuzer for the lessons – just enough to pay for his own.

Amon (who later also taught Josef and Eduard) told Johann that the *Stehgeiger* – the violinist standing in front of the orchestra playing the fiddle and conducting with his bow – is the star of the orchestra. He must look well and play well. Amon taught Johann to practise in front of a mirror in order to have an elegant bow stroke and to watch his posture and his movements.

At the age of eleven Johann entered the Schottengymnasium which remains one of Vienna's most prestigious secondary schools. He was not a bad pupil, but he was more interested in his violin than in Latin or Greek. When his father found him practising in front of the mirror one day he took the violin away and strictly forbade him to continue. But his mother gave him – again secretly – one of his father's violins, and he went on playing.

After four years at the Gymnasium he was enrolled at a commercial-technical school to learn business correspondence and the mysteries of double-entry bookkeeping. A friend of his father, a bank manager, had promised to take the boy. If he worked well all his life, he might retire with a pension. What could be better?

Johann stuck it out for two years, always going back to his violin when his father was away. The only part of the curriculum he liked was the weekly singing lesson. One day the boy sitting next to him – Gustav Lewy, later court music publisher, who remained one of Strauss's closest friends – asked Johann to sing for him a melody from the book, 'but softly'. Johann began *pianissimo*, but was soon carried away and suddenly sang *forte*. The teacher was furious. There was a scandal, and Johann was thrown out of school. His father did not give up, however: a private tutor was hired, Ludwig Scheyrer – who also loved music.

After Johann Strauss had moved out of the Hirschenhaus to live with Emilie, there was no sense in pretending that his eldest son would become a bank clerk. Johann wrote a moving letter to his father. He had decided, 'after summoning all the strength of my heart and spirit for this step, so important for the future of my mother, who might be left without protection and help . . . to show her my gratitude at least by trying to achieve something in my profession'. Music, of course. He asked his father please to understand 'that I shall remain on my mother's side'. He signed the letter, 'with respect and love your devoted son, Johann Strauss'. He was eighteen. He knew the family could not depend on their father's support. Very soon he would have to start earning money to support his mother, his sisters and brothers.

Once the decision was made, the young man devoted his life to his chosen profession. He studied the violin with Johann Anton Kohlmann, a ballet master at the Kärnthnertortheater. Kohlmann had been his mother's choice. At that time ballets were rehearsed with a single violinist playing the melody from the score. Anna Strauss decided that a good ballet master would be the best teacher for a dance musician. Strauss also studied theory with Joseph Drechsler, a noted church composer. As a boy Drechsler had seen Mozart. Later he had tried his hand at everything. He had been conductor at the Josephstadt Theater and had written the music for some of Ferdinand Raimund's beautiful fairy-tale plays. He also wrote the lovely, melancholy song *Brüderlein fein . . . es muss geschieden sein* (My

dear brother … one day one must go). He died in 1852 as much honoured
Domkapellmeister of St Stephen's.

Drechsler meant well, trying to guide his gifted pupil towards the
wonderful mysteries of church music. Strauss worked on a *Kyrie*, but
his heart was not in it; he had some problems 'with diminished and
augmented triads'. Once, when he was doing some organ practice
and thought he was alone, he began to intersperse a fugue with a
polka melody.

Drechsler was exasperated. 'Aus Ihnen wird nix' ('You won't get
anywhere') he said. Strauss made a serious effort. He wrote a
Gradual, *Tu qui regis totum orbem*, for four voices and wind instruments,
and Drechsler liked it well enough to have it performed at the Kirche
am Hof. After a year, however, Strauss told him he was going to be a
dance musician. Drechsler seems to have understood. He even gave
the boy a nice testimonial: 'Having found Johann a modest and
intelligent boy, I do hope that his talent will be furthered as much as
possible.'

Strauss enclosed the testimonial, together with one from Ballet-
master Kohlmann, and the score of the Gradual with his application
to the magistrate asking for a licence 'to perform dance music, opera
selections and concert pieces, depending on the demands', and under-

took to pay twenty florins as employment tax. Making music was considered a 'free profession', for which a minor did not need his parents' consent. It is doubtful whether his father would have given it. Johann received his licence early in September 1844.

Johann Strauss began forming his orchestra of twenty-four men at the inn Zur Stadt Belgrad, the hangout of unemployed musicians. Contracts were signed on 8 October. Now he had the musicians, but he had hardly time to form an orchestra; it had taken his father several years to attain perfection 'by thorough study and continuous rehearsing'.

To find a place for his debut was a serious problem. The proprietors of the most important establishments were afraid of offending Father Strauss, and turned the boy down. At last, Anna Strauss went to see the mayor of Hietzing, a lovely suburb near Schönbrunn, and it was agreed that Johann would make his debut at Dommayer's Casino.

On 12 October the surprised Viennese read in the *Wiener Zeitung*:

Today Saturday grand soirée of Herr Capellmeister Johann Strauss at Sperl's.
Tomorrow Sunday great soirée at Lindenbauer's Casino in Simmering. The orchestra of the late J. Lanner.
Invitation to a soirée dansante taking place on Tuesday, 15 October 1844, even in inclement weather, at Dommayer's Casino in Hietzing. Johann Strauss (Son) has the honour of conducting for the first time his own orchestra, performing various overtures and opera pieces, and several of his own compositions. To the favour and grace of the esteemed public he recommends himself faithfully.

Johann Strauss jun.

By showing respect for his father and for Lanner by including them in his own advertisement, Strauss tried to soften up his enemies, but the announcement caused a first-class sensation in Vienna. The waltz king of Vienna, challenged by his own son, not yet nineteen! The father was quoted as saying, 'Goodness, now the lad wants to write waltzes of which he hasn't the faintest idea! It isn't even easy for me, after all these years, to create something new in eight or twelve bars.'

One might have expected the Viennese to have had other worries. There was talk of revolution throughout the Habsburg Empire. In Vienna the poor were getting terribly poor, and the rich were scandalously rich. Metternich's police were more ruthless than ever. Nevertheless the announcement of the debut of young Strauss was the biggest news in the waltz-crazy city. There were other good waltz orchestras – Fahrbach, Morelly, Bendel, Ballin. Each waltz composer had his fans. But this time it was Strauss versus Strauss. The father's partisans and most music critics ridiculed the son's

A page of the *Wiener Zeitung* on 12 October, 1844 with Strauss's advertisement sandwiched between one for his father and one for Lanner's orchestra.

RIGHT A view of Vienna from Grinzing by Karl Agricola.

'impertinence'. A Viennese dance conductor was expected to perform his own music, but young Strauss was admitting that he had written only four waltzes, three polkas and two quadrilles. How dared he?

It was reported that Father Strauss was quite bitter about Dommayer letting his son perform there. Had they forgotten that only ten years earlier, the elder Strauss had performed there his *Elizabethan Waltz*, Op. 71, for the first time? The critics had called it 'one of his best'. Dommayer's Casino, across the street from the Schönbrunn Park, was an elegant building with a classical, Imperial-yellow façade in the style of Karl Friedrich Schinkel, with columns and frieze. There was a restaurant with a dance and concert hall, much less pretentious than Sperl's.

It must have been difficult to get a table on the afternoon of Tuesday, 15 October. Everybody who was anybody in Vienna wanted to be there at six o'clock. Some hoped for a success, some for a flop: all were curious. 'Dommayer's had never seen anything like it', writes Ada B. Teetgen. 'The police got nasty when important individuals made too free with their elbows. Women got hurt and fainted.' The concert hall with its ornamental stucco ceiling and beautiful chandeliers was overcrowded, mostly with supporters of the elder Strauss. He wasn't there; instead he had sent his friends Hirsch and Haslinger. In a corner in the back a nervous woman was sitting. No one paid attention to her. It was Anna Strauss.

Johann Strauss appeared on the platform, elegant, pale, black-haired ('Just like his father', some people said), wearing a dark-blue tailcoat with silver buttons, and a silk waistcoat with hand-embroidered flowers. (The papers had reported that the tailor had not been paid yet.) The young man had terrible stage fright, and he did not feel better when Haslinger, leader of his father's supporters, signalled at them to hiss. However, others present applauded, and it was some time before the orchestra could play the first piece, the overture of Auber's *La Muette de Portici*. The second piece was a composition of young Strauss, his waltz *Die Gunstwerber* (freely translated, *Please, like me!*). It had to be four times repeated: they definitely did like the waltz. Afterwards Strauss played and conducted *Herzenslust Polka*, *Debut Quadrille*, and another waltz, *Sinngedichte*. There was bedlam: without doubt Vienna had a new star. At the end the son conquered even his enemies when he performed his father's most popular waltz, *Loreley-Rhein-Klänge*. Many women were crying. Later that night Strauss and his mother were crying too – with happiness.

The poet Johann Nepomuk Vogl wrote in *Österreichische Wochen-zeitung*, 'Talent is no one's monopoly, it can be inherited. . . . The young man has the same flow of melody and the same piquant instru-mentation as the father yet he does not slavishly imitate the father's

Johann Strauss playing the
violin at his first performance in
Dommayer's Casino in 1844.

style', and the acid commentator M.G.Saphir had recorded a 'victory
and triumph'. The *Wanderer*'s critic, Wiest, had left Dommayer's at
midnight 'after the orchestra had repeated *Sinngedichte* for the nineteenth time'. As his cab passed the empty house, The Cock, where
Lanner had died the year before, Wiest thought, 'Up there another
Viennese wrote some pretty good waltzes. Good night, Lanner!
Good evening, Strauss Father! Good morning, Strauss Son!' Wiest
may be forgotten, but his greeting is not.

And in the morning Hirsch went to see Father Strauss and reported
not happily but truthfully, 'The rascal was terrific.'

Suddenly the proprietors of all fancy establishments who had
recently turned down the younger Strauss, wanted him to perform at
their places. Three nights after Dommayer's the young man performed at Lindenbauer's Casino in Simmering, then in the Prater
and in other dance halls. Once again Vienna's waltz *aficionados* were
split, as in the early days of Lanner and the first Strauss. To have one
prima donna is fine, but to have two is better.

On 11 November the elder Strauss tacitly recognized his competitor. That day big posters said, 'Kapellmeister Strauss (Father)

conducts the music.' Some newspapers reported that the elder Strauss had increased his orchestra to 220 men, 'which proves that he is still Vienna's favourite', and others that 'young Strauss is modest, unassuming and happy when some of the favour, justly due to his father, will be accorded to him.' Another paper stated diplomatically, 'During the next *Fasching* the beautiful women of Vienna will dance to the sounds of two Strauss fiddles.'

Young Strauss was already a star, and there were the inevitable stories. He had performed for an impoverished actor. He gave a special concert in aid of some people in Sievering whose house had burned down. And there was a romantic legend about one Reserl Strüber with whom he had been in love and who had died. 'He guilded the last hours of her short life with the sweet melodies of his violin.' And somebody wrote, brutally, that his father was finished.

No man likes to be told that he is old and finished – certainly not a much admired, distinguished waltz composer at the age of forty-three. There were the usual cliques and intrigues, and the pride and vanity of the elder Strauss was hurt. He seemed to derive no satisfaction from the fact that it was his own son who had inherited his talent and fame. The young man continued to perform his father's music – not for cheap sentimental effect but because he genuinely admired his father.

Eventually they met, and talked things over. The father was still autocratic, the son was respectful. The misunderstandings, created by gossip and intrigue, were discussed and settled. But when the father suggested that his son should join his own orchestra as deputy and concertmaster, the son declined, regretfully but firmly. His father understood: the boy's mother stood between them, and he had no right to insist. They shook hands, and each went his way. It was a truce but no real peace; their respective followers would not let them have peace.

In 1847 Wilhelm von Kaulbach wrote to his wife, 'Vienna is a city of sensuous pleasures, and Strauss the sun around which everything turns.' He did not say which Strauss. In those last days before the March Revolution the Viennese waltz fans had a fine time. The sky was filled with Strauss violins. One could hear the elder Strauss at Sperl's, Zeisig's, the Sieben Kurfürsten; or his son at Dommayer's, Zögernitz, the Sträusselsäle. During military parades the father directed the band of the First Regiment of the Citizens' Guard (red uniforms) while the younger Strauss had been appointed to Lanner's post as band master of the Second Regiment (blue uniforms).

On special occasions the band masters would march with their regiments, salute one another, conduct the same march, salute and leave again. It was a fine spectacle for their fans, but not an easy experience for father and son; much tact was needed. Vienna was just too small for two Strauss orchestras. The father sensed this. He often went on tour during these difficult years.

On 8 January 1845 Father Strauss conducted his *Odeon Tänze*, Opus 172, for the opening of a palatial new establishment, the Odeon. Why a new showplace was needed, no one could explain, not even the foolhardy people who financed it. Perhaps they thought the Viennese always wanted something new in the way of entertainment, and they were not entirely wrong. The opening was a big success. 'Between two winter gardens with eight thousand flowers was the large dance hall for ten thousand people, lit by several hundredweights of candles.' Peter Fischer, the owner, had installed mirrors, fountains and a billiard room. Unfortunately he forgot to build a smoking room. The young men lighted their cigars in the ballroom which bothered the ladies. The food was bad, there were not enough waiters, and only 'every tenth guest' was served. Fischer soon corrected the short-comings. Two weeks later the papers wrote that fifteen thousand people went to the Odeon to dance to the elder Strauss's music. He had increased his already large orchestra 'to be heard in the immense ballroom'.

The glory of the Odeon was shortlived. Early in 1846 Fischer announced in the *Wiener Zeitung* that he would sell his enterprise 'as a whole or in parts, as inn, pastry shop etc'. He was ruined.

In July 1846 a special event took place in the Brühl, a suburb of Mödling. *Hofballmusikdirektor* Strauss would perform the *Hungarian Storm March* by Liszt. 'Herr Franz Liszt will perform around eight o'clock some solo pieces on the pianoforte.' Some critics said it was a silly idea 'because the wind would carry away the sound'. But Liszt insisted; the net proceeds of the concert were for a new clock for the tower of nearby Rodaun where Liszt liked to spend his summers. Strauss's orchestra performed at the beginning and at the end, and in between Liszt 'played magnificently'. Of the proceeds of 500 florins, 330 were used for the installation of the new clock.

People in Vienna wondered why the younger Strauss performed so many of his father's compositions. Decsey calls it 'a subconscious longing for harmony'. Fifty years later Siegmund Freud might have considered that the son found in his father's music the warmth and tenderness he had missed in the man. To the end of his life Strauss had a deep affection for his father and genuine admiration for him as a composer, 'a musician by the grace of God'.

He also followed his father's example when he performed new music in his concerts. The elder Strauss had played Mozart, Beethoven, Weber, Cherubini, Mendelssohn and Meyerbeer. The son played much Liszt and introduced Wagner in Vienna. Long before the

ABOVE The interior of the
Odeon ballroom depicted
on a music cover.

RIGHT An entrance ticket
to the Odeon.

Kärnthnertortheater performed *Tannhäuser* and *Lohengrin*, Strauss had performed selections from the operas in his Volksgarten concerts.

He had not inherited his father's restless ways, however. He never liked travel, although some touring was necessary to prove to the Viennese that he was accepted elsewhere. In the early weeks of 1848 he took his band to Serbia and Romania. They wore the blue uniforms of the Citizens' Guard Regiment which impressed the uniform-conscious Balkans. In Bucharest a deputation of Austrian residents asked Strauss to relieve the Austrian Consul from office. The young man complied – later it was said he had had too much champagne – and a report of the incident reached Metternich in Vienna. But the young man was already very popular, and the police did not bother with him; they had more serious problems. Once again it was *Fasching*, and people were dancing, but in the poorer suburbs the bakers' shops were plundered, 'while Vienna's intoxicated rich cheered young Strauss's *Bacchus* Polka at the Sofiensäle'. People who claimed they had no money to pay their taxes would cheerfully pawn their watches for a ticket at Sperl's where the elder Strauss was playing. Some were singing, 'Sell my clothes, I'm going to heaven. . . .'

And then came news from Paris where the Second Republic had been proclaimed on the barricades on 24 February 1848. In Vienna the great balls continued. When the explosion started in the waltz capital of Europe, no one was more surprised than many Viennese.

6
1848: Father against Sons

The Viennese Revolution of 1848, 'in essence . . . a liberal idea that failed' (R. John Rath), was a disaster for Vienna and Austria. For many people it was a family tragedy, a generation problem. Among the most prominent were the two Strausses. 1848 created an abyss which they could never bridge over.

The Viennese Revolution was a baroque affair which lasted seven and a half months. It began on 13 March when students, burghers and workers demonstrated at the Ständehaus, demanding freedom of the Press, freedom of science and the resignation of Metternich. Soldiers fired into the crowd. Thirty were killed. That night Metternich resigned and left Vienna the next day. There was widespread elation. Grillparzer called it 'the gayest revolution imaginable. Favoured by beautiful spring weather, the whole population filled the streets all day long.'

The elation was short-lived. After the hasty departure of Metternich Emperor Ferdinand made a somewhat more dignified exit to Innsbruck. A second revolt swept Vienna in May, but no one in the city talked of victory: the Revolution got nowhere. The revolutionaries wrangled in the polyglot assembly, and could agree on nothing. The Revolution was already devouring its own children. The Emperor had returned. Only in Germany was Vienna still the big hope among the radicals. Wagner in Dresden wrote 'Greeting from Saxony', a bad poem, full of admiration for the Viennese. Early in October fighting broke out between the Black-Yellows, the anti-revolutionary, pro-Establishment National Guard units, and the radical sections. Soldiers were sent to restore order, the War Ministry was stormed, and Count Latour, the War Minister, was hanged from a lamp-post in fine French revolutionary style. The Emperor ran away again, this time making a rather undignified exit to Olmütz (Olomouc), the Moravian fortress. From there he ordered the Croat nationalist, General Banus Jellačić, to move his troops against Vienna. Field-Marshal Prince Alfred Windischgrätz, who had shelled and occupied Prague in June, was made supreme commander in the fight against insurgent Vienna.

Vienna refused to capitulate. The insurgents, over fifty thousand, went down fighting against the forces of Windischgrätz and Jellačić. They never had a chance. By 31 October the soldiers of Windischgrätz had occupied all of Vienna, and retribution began.

When the Revolution had started, the elder Strauss was forty-four, much admired by his public – conservative burghers, army officers and generally Black-Yellow partisans of the monarchy. He had always been a conservative, but it would not be fair to call him a reactionary, or to call his sons, Johann and Josef, revolutionaries. The boys were young; they hated the Metternich regime; above all they wanted to protest against all that was old. But they were not politically minded; neither was their father. In the Strauss family life had always moved around music: nothing else mattered. Their weapons were fiddle and bow, and their ammunition was melodies. In the preface to his father's Collected Works, Johann Strauss wrote, 'My father's art was at its zenith during the *Fasching* of 1848. . . . The artistic idyll was interrupted by the storms of the March days. They deeply depressed my father. His artistic soul couldn't thrive in the noise of those days.'

Father Strauss made it obvious – some said, too obvious – where he stood. He would play, rather demonstratively, dance music for the Establishment. On a warm night, on 31 August 1848, he gave a soirée at the Water-Glacis (today the Stadtpark), a popular rendezvous of army officers and monarchists. Young people rarely went there. At the Water-Glacis Strauss had had one of his great triumphs with *Loreley-Rhein-Klänge* five years previously. That night his friend Hirsch had placed his bulbs and flames strategically. Suddenly a big picture of Field-Marshal Radetzky, showing him on his horse, was revealed.

Radetzky, commander of the Imperial Forces in Italy, had defeated Charles Albert of Piedmont at Custozza, put down the 'insurgent democrats' in Milan, and then he had conquered Verona. He spent his last years as Governor of Lombardy and the Veneto at the Villa Reale in Milan. He remained there after being pensioned, and died in 1858 at the age of eighty-two.

That August night at the Water-Glacis Strauss performed Beethoven's *Leonore* Overture No. 3 and three of his waltzes. Afterwards he conducted his latest composition, *Radetzky March*, Opus 228. It was an immediate success, and had to be repeated three times. General Zanoni, whose major military achievement was his 'reform' which permitted officers to wear moustaches, got up and demanded a fourth

OPPOSITE A cartoon of Metternich's flight from Vienna in 1848.

96

repetition. Applause and cheers. The *Radetzky March* became at once the spiritual hymn of the Austrian soldiers, just as the younger Strauss's *The Blue Danube* later became the spiritual anthem of all Austrians.

The *Radetzky March* has lost none of its appeal and remains the masterpiece of the first Strauss. At the annual New Year's Concert of the Vienna Philharmonic, *The Blue Danube Waltz* is the first, and the *Radetzky March* the second and last encore. It outlived the popularity of all waltzes by the elder Strauss.

Ironically it was at Sperl's, the Black-Yellow loyalist citadel of Father Strauss, where a meeting of the Democratic Society on

The Strauss family were divided by the revolution in 1848. The elder Strauss supported the old order and wrote one of his finest works, *Radetzky March*, in honour of the general. His sons' sympathies lay with the revolutionaries and Johann played his *Revolution March* at the barricades.

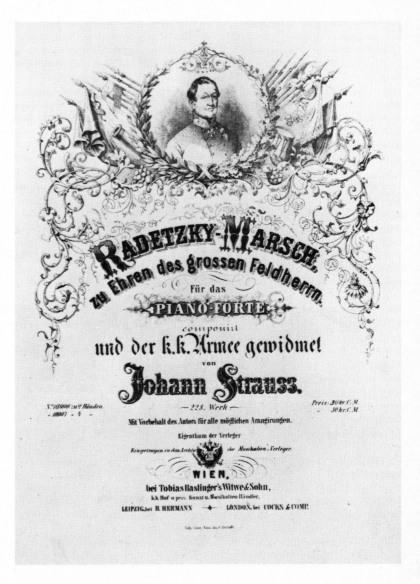

5 October demanded abolition of the monarchy, proclamation of the Republic and complete 'social revolution'. That was high treason. According to the *Theaterzeitung* the violent events of October that culminated with the lynching of War Minister Latour began at Sperl's. At the University Robert Blum, the delegate of the Frankfurt Parliament, demanded that five hundred other reactionaries be 'Latourized'. Blum was later executed. Some optimists said that insurgent troops were arriving from Hungary; that the Revolution was 'almost' won. It was not. After Windischgrätz occupied the city, everybody took off his uniform and put on his top hat 'to be recognized from far away as a loyal citizen'. On 2 December Emperor

Ferdinand renounced his throne in favour of his eighteen-year-old nephew. The reign of Franz Joseph I had begun.

Things must really have been bad. Even Father Strauss played to almost empty ballrooms at the Sofiensäle and the Elysium. For once the Viennese did not feel like making merry. On 13 February 1849 Strauss played the *Wanderers Lebewohl Waltz*, Opus 237, and went on tour again. He made the mistake of going to Prague where Windischgrätz had recently turned his guns against the Old Town. Strauss was booed and ridiculed. He made another mistake when he went to Germany. In Heilbronn and Heidelberg the students showed their contempt by marching in front of his hotel wearing black-yellow caps. His concerts were boycotted. In Frankfurt the people demonstratively shouted 'Berlioz!'. The French composer had written the revolutionary *Rákoczy March*, glorifying the Hungarian patriot. Strauss was deeply depressed, and decided to try England where he had been happy eleven years ago.

On 26 April *The Morning Post* in London wrote, 'If the revolutionary mania of Austria has unsettled Germany, at least England has no reason to lament the political mischief, for no doubt to this circumstance are we indebted for Strauss's presence amongst us.' Later *The Times* reported a performance of Strauss and his orchestra at a court ball in Buckingham Palace on 30 April. Strauss had presented his *Alice Polka*.

He also went to pay his respects to Metternich. Once the most powerful and most hated man in Europe, he now lived in London as a refugee. His wife and daughter burst into tears when Strauss came to see them. Only over a year ago he had played for them at a court ball in the Redoutensaal. Princess Melanie was very bitter; she told Strauss the Viennese were suffering what they deserved – civil war and economic misery.

Many Viennese said that Strauss had shown very bad taste in going to see Metternich. He received threatening letters. Didn't he know that among many others Hermann Jellinek, a musician, and Alfred Julius Becher, a popular composer, had been executed during the reign of terror that followed the Revolution?

He seemed to have lost his sense of judgement. He received invitations from Queen Victoria and from some of the Tories, but many other people ignored him pointedly. Lots of liberals sympathized with the German republicans, and especially with the Hungarians who had unsuccessfully revolted against the Habsburgs. At a concert in Exeter Hall on 14 May Strauss 'performed several of his most esteemed waltzes', according to *The Times*. Jetty Treffz, a Viennese singer, sang several Austrian songs and was much applauded after *Home Sweet Home*, which later became a popular encore of

The last portrait of a tired and disillusioned Metternich in 1859.

Adelina Patti and Nellie Melba. By that time, Treffz had become the first wife of Johann Strauss Son.

On 5 July *The Morning Post* reported that 'a numerous party of the *haut ton* formed themselves into a committee to arrange a farewell matinée musicale for the Maestro'. Afterwards the musicians played the melancholy song from Raimund's *Alpenkönig und Menschenfeind*; '*So leb denn woh', du stilles Haus*'. A lot of people were crying.

Johann and Josef Strauss had been on the side of the insurgents from the beginning of the Revolution. While their father was playing dance music in loyalist circles, Johann stopped playing and writing waltzes. He wanted to express his opposition to the regime the only way he could do it – in his music. He wrote marches and polkas with titles that made it clear where he stood. The engraved cover of the *Revolution March* showed students and members of the National Guard (the former Citizens' Guard) in heroic poses on a barricade made of pavement stones. While Karl Beck, the social poet of the pre-March, wrote his indictments of the ruling class, young Strauss wrote the *Students' March*, which was published as Opus 56, but immediately confiscated by the police. Other works of that time were the *Freiheitslieder, Burschenlieder* and *Song of the Barricades*.

Young Johann, a member of the National Guard, had to wear uniform, drill and do regular duty. 'Though he never had great enthusiasm for the uniform, he accepted the "patriotic condition"', the biographer Eisenberg writes with obvious embarrassment. On 22 August, a very hot day, Strauss was on sentry duty in Karmeliter-gasse. Suddenly there was shooting nearby. He was ordered to alert the members of his unit. A workers' riot had started in the Leopold-stadt district, and the unit would have 'to suppress the disturbance'.

H. E. Jacob suggests that Strauss did not care about the Revolution. Others have suggested that he would not fight against the workers. At any rate he ignored his orders, placed his rifle inside the sentry hut – and went home to his mother. He was hungry – all biographers agree on *that*. Anna Strauss gave him something to eat. He now felt fine, and began composing some music. That was *his* contribution to the Revolution. As late as October, however, when there was widespread fighting in Vienna and many revolutionaries had some sober second thoughts and disappeared for a while, Strauss took his band to the barricades. They played the *Revolution March* and the greatest revolutionary song of all, *La Marseillaise*, 'accompanying the concert of the flying bullets' (Eisenberg). 'Had he been killed then, he would hardly have died for the Revolution but rather for his own intoxication and for beautiful music' (Jacob).

Fortunately he was not killed during the fighting. He showed character and courage when he was interrogated by the police on

6 December. According to the police record he admitted having played *La Marseillaise* at a time when this was foolhardy, for the brutal soldiers of Jellačić arrested many and killed some for no reason at all. Why shouldn't he play *La Marseillaise*, Strauss asked the police. He had always played music that had 'an essential value'. He said, 'At the Grünes Tor [Green Gate] *La Marseillaise* was demanded. . . . To avoid trouble I had to give in. We even had to repeat it. There was much applause, but some people hissed.' He was not punished, but a police record was attached to his file. This may have delayed his appointment as *Hofballmusikdirektor* until 1863.

Why wasn't he prosecuted? Perhaps the police officials secretly liked the young waltz composer. He was very popular. And even among the authorities there were those who had secret sympathy with many of the revolutionaries' demands. It was also noted that Strauss had shown 'the proper attitude' four days earlier. On 2 December, the young Franz Joseph 1 had been crowned Emperor following the abdication of Ferdinand. In honour of the young Emperor, Strauss 'conducted his band in a stirring performance of his father's *Radetzky March*', which had also 'essential value' as a piece of music. 'Later young Strauss repeatedly demonstrated his affection for the Emperor and members of the Imperial house, and the sun of Imperial favour rose again,' writes Eisenberg, strictly a Black-Yellow man.

Josef Strauss had his problems, too. As a student of the Polytechnic he had joined the Academic Legion early in March, and fought with it during the long months, right to the bitter end. Afterwards he resumed his civilian clothes and continued his studies. Somebody denounced him. Five Polish soldiers came to the Hirschenhaus and tried to arrest Josef. Anna Strauss dealt with them efficiently. She had not been actively on the side of the revolutionaries, but she wouldn't permit the brutal soldiers of the Windischgrätz army to get hold of her second boy. Josef was hidden, the soldiers received some money, and left.

After his return from England Father Strauss appeared at Unger's Casino in Hernals, and was received, 'as usual, with rapturous delight' by his Black-Yellow followers. 'The good spirit of our merriment has returned at the right moment,' wrote the *Theaterzeitung*. Less than eight months after the October tragedy, Vienna was Vienna again, 'Sell my clothes, I'm going to heaven'. Infected by the widespread enthusiasm Strauss blundered and wrote his *Jellačić March*, dedicated to that hated Croat nationalist general who had publicly vowed 'to lock up the Viennese in a fool's tower' and 'to dictate the Black-Yellow peace with my sabre'. Even among the loyalist followers of the regime he was discredited and hated.

Some of Strauss's most ardent admirers thought he had lost his senses when he first performed it on 16 September. Something strange also happened: as Strauss was about to play the first notes, he broke his bow. The incident, then hardly noticed, was later counted an ill omen.

On 19 September Strauss appeared at Sperl's and gave a successful concert. For Saturday, 22 September, a State banquet in honour of Field-Marshal Radetzky was scheduled. Strauss, the Radetzky glorifier, was to conduct the orchestra. He began composing a *Radetzky Banquet March*. It is now called *Letzter Gedanke (Last Thought)*, Opus 252. The autograph shows twenty completed bars, four partially orchestrated and some sketchy hints – it then breaks off. At the end Carl Haslinger wrote, 'During the instrumentation Father Strauss came down with scarlet fever and died three days later.'

Strauss had caught the infection from one of his daughters by Emilie Trambusch in Kumpfgasse. Meningitis was the fatal complication. He died around two o'clock on the morning of 25 September.

Josef Strauss heard about his father's death quite by accident later that morning. He ran into Kumpfgasse where 'he found his father's dead body in an empty room'. This is the version given in Eduard Strauss's *Memoirs*. 'My father was lying on the wooden boards that had been removed from the bed and placed on the floor. The bed had already disappeared, and with it everything in the room and in the flat that wasn't nailed down. . . .'

Eduard is not always an objective witness, however, especially when Emilie Trambusch is concerned. According to another version Anna Strauss and her children 'ran across the Danube Canal into Kumpfgasse, past large posters announcing the personal appearance of *Hofballmusikdirektor* Johann Strauss at the Radetzky Banquet'. Jäger-Sunstenau, a reliable source, writes, 'Shortly after the death of Johann Strauss, the magistrate sent a commissioner to seal the apartment. The commissioner's inventory mentions a complete set of furniture.' The list, dated 2 October 1849, No 73.543, is long and detailed.

Emilie Trambusch had gone, taking her children with her, and Strauss's sons had great difficulty in getting their father's instruments and scores from her. Only on 23 March 1852 was a settlement of the estate signed by Anna Strauss, Emilie Trambusch, Johann and Josef Strauss, and Carl Haslinger. There were rumours that Emilie had beaten 'half-dead' the little girl from whom Strauss had caught his last illness. Emilie later disappeared in poverty and misery. It is ironic that Vienna's idol made his way from a run-down tavern in Flossgasse to the palaces of emperors and queens, only to die in a dark tenement flat in Kumpfgasse.

Strauss had a magnificent funeral, the sort of super-spectacle he would have enjoyed very much. The chroniclers noted approvingly that it was 'almost as magnificent as Beethoven's'. The bill for the funeral included 155 guilders for the priest in Oberdöbling, 55 guilders for the regimental band, 87 guilder to the wax merchant Karl Bach for candles, 72 guilders for obituary notices. Johann Strauss wrote that 'over a hundred thousand people had come to pay the last homage'. Every fourth Viennese was in the streets watching the funeral procession. The coffin was carried by members of his orchestra. Behind the coffin Franz Amon, the old leader of the orchestra, walked carrying the Master's violin on a black cushion. Its strings had been cut. Everybody broke into tears. It was a fine funeral, almost as much fun as when the *Herr Hofballmusikdirektor* had performed a new waltz. Two military bands and Fahrbach's orchestra played a funeral march that Carl Haslinger had arranged, 'after motives of Johann Strauss's last waltz, *Wanderers Lebewohl*'. Many people said that *Wanderer's Goodbye* had been Strauss's foreboding of his own death. 'Not at all,' writes Karl Reinöhl. 'Strauss never thought of the possibility of dying. But he had been depressed by the political situation and the competition of his gifted son. And he had guilt feelings about his family at the Hirschenhaus.'

The members of the Männergesangverein sang two choruses, while Johann Strauss was buried at Döbling Cemetery next to his old friend and erstwhile competitor, Joseph Lanner. The *mise-en-scène* was perfect, 'not one eye remained without tears'. Eduard von Bauernfeld, the 'radical' poet who had not agreed with Strauss's political opinions, wrote a long poem, *Das Leben ein Tanz (Life is a dance)*: 'Poor Vienna! The gods love you no more for they took your best – your Strauss. . . . The old, fat Vienna, the Falstaff among the German cities . . . was buried today.'

In Paris Berlioz wrote, 'I can still see him as he conducted on the gallery of the beautiful Redoutensaal, and hundreds of beautiful Viennese women, caught by the bacchantic lust of dance and melody, obeyed his rhythms. In the pauses they applauded him enthusiastically. With Strauss Vienna lost one of its most beautiful ornaments.'

Much later his son wrote in the preface to his father's Collected Works, 'He spread the fame of dance music around the globe. Strict judges have not denied him their recognition. . . .'

Fifty-six years after the death of the first Strauss the Viennese put up a monument in Döbling Cemetery. It shows the two old friends, Lanner and Strauss, standing next to each other.

Two days after his father's funeral, on 2 October, Johann Strauss conducted his father's orchestra for the first time in the Colonnade of the Volksgarten. Publisher Haslinger had composed a *Nachruf an Strauss Vater*, a musical obituary. Later there was a memorial concert

OPPOSITE A Seressaner, one of Jellačić's brutal soldiers.

Goebel

at the Sofiensäle ending with the *Radetzky March*. It was all very nice, but insiders knew that there had been grave problems. Several members of the orchestra had refused to perform 'under the rebel'. Many Viennese suddenly became ardent partisans of the father and accused the son 'of failing to show filial piety'. The supporters of the son said that 'he had been forced into a struggle with the dead'. It was a bizarre situation with sinister undertones, very Viennese. Everybody had a fine time except the young man himself. He had been quite happy performing with his own orchestra. Suddenly he was considered a dark intriguer and scheming pretender, quite against his own will. There was even talk of boycotting him. Strauss had to appeal to public opinion. In the *Wiener Zeitung* he explained that at the age of twenty-four he had to support his mother, two sisters and two brothers. Anna and Theresa were twenty and eighteen; Josef and Eduard, twenty-two and fourteen, were both students. He concluded his appeal, 'I feel my dear father's influence is with me. It leads me to the spirit that mourns at his grave. I shall show myself worthy of him.'

Vienna was appeased. After a while the matter died down. The penitent orchestral members were told to play or leave. They stayed.

Strauss continued to live with the family at the Hirschenhaus. He was rarely at home except for a few hours of sleep. He had inherited the position and the duties of his father: he was now the only Strauss. He had to perform everywhere and to compose for everybody. The Strauss enterprise expanded into a large organization. At first Strauss had two orchestras, then three and finally four. All concerts announced his personal appearance which created problems. He would use a *Fiaker* – a coach drawn by two horses – to get from one place to the next, play a couple of dances, and on to his next engagement. Vienna was a large city, and there were wide distances to be traversed. Strauss's weekly programme reads almost like the schedules of great conductors and singers today. On Monday he would be at Dommayer's in Hietzing where he had started his career. On Tuesday at the Volksgarten. On Wednesday at Grüner Zeisig. On Thursday at Valentin's Beer Hall, later called Zobel. On Friday again at the Volksgarten. On Saturday at Engländer's Restauration. On Sunday at Unger's Casino in Hernals. 'No foreigner left Vienna without having heard Strauss's waltzes under the composer's direction,' wrote Eisenberg. 'To miss such an event would be like going to Rome without seeing the Vatican.'

The young man was a practising musician – violinist and conductor. He was also the head of a large business organization. And he had to compose, all the time. How he found the peace of mind needed to create is hard to imagine, but he wrote good music in these hectic years. There were other waltz composers in Vienna, and Strauss had

OPPOSITE Two scenes from the revolution of 1848. LEFT Viennese students manning the barricades. ABOVE The troops of Field Marshal Windischgrätz bombard the city.

to prove himself with each new work. The critics wrote long articles about a new waltz.

In his preface to his father's works Strauss wrote:

Composing was perhaps easier in his time than it is now. To write a polka today one has to study the entire musical literature and possibly some philosophical systems. In the old days it was sufficient 'to have an idea'. Strangely one always had one. Our self-confidence was such that we would often announce a new waltz for the evening, though not one note had been written in the morning. In such a case the orchestra appeared at the composer's home. As soon as one part of the waltz was composed, the musicians would arrange and copy the music. Meanwhile the miracle of 'the idea' would repeat itself. A few hours later the whole piece was ready, was rehearsed, and would be performed in the evening for an enthusiastic audience.

There were balls for every social group and occasion. M.G. Saphir, the influential critic, differentiates between public balls, *redoutes*, closed-society balls for certain privileged strata (the court, the diplomats, the military), house balls, *piqueniques*, and *Schnackerlbälle* for the lower classes – who were often better behaved than their superiors. The house balls were an ordeal for wealthy fathers. For weeks prior to the terrifying event the household routine was disrupted. Only cold meals were served while oil lamps and candlesticks were cleaned, and women fainted when a new dress did not fit. For all the expense and discomfort the father got only the vague hope of marrying off one of his daughters. Enormous buffets were arranged for hungry bachelors who came, ate and drank, and sometimes did not even bother to dance with the daughters but gave their attentions to some attractive, probably married woman.

And there were high-society balls, the rendezvous of the Upper Five Hundred. The number of tickets was limited and announced in the newspapers. The tickets were sold in coffee-houses only to persons of rank. These élite balls had strict laws. Often they opened with a Chopin Polonaise, then came waltzes and polkas. The third dance preceding the supper would be a quadrille. Afterwards the women had the privilege of asking the men for a waltz which led to dramatic complications. Then there would be more waltzes and fast polkas. The programme of the Concordia Ball, of 19 February 1906, features fifteen waltzes, ten polkas and eight quadrilles, and many dances were repeated, often several times. The *Fasching* was a season for well-trained athletes.

After the middle of the century life was beautiful for Strauss. He was young – in his late twenties – gifted and ambitious. At the Hirschenhaus his mother took good care of him. He got along well with his brothers and sisters. There was no more tension in the

OPPOSITE The memorial to Strauss and Lanner in Döbling Cemetery.

STRAVSS · LANNER

family. His only regret was that the day had only twenty-four hours. He was in demand all over Vienna. He was popular everywhere, except at the court where it was well remembered that the 'red' Strauss had written some 'dangerous' music in 1848. The Emperor himself was said to have decided against Strauss as his father's successor in the position of *Hofballmusikdirektor*. Franz Joseph I did not easily forget and forgive. In 1850, and again in 1856, Strauss submitted requests which were turned down by the *Obersthofmeisteramt*.

Nevertheless it was occasionally difficult to get along without young Strauss. In May 1852 he performed at a 'déjeuner in the glass houses'. The bill exists: Strauss was paid 9 guilders; each of the 40 *Individuen* (as the musicians were called) got 4.30. Once an archduchess demanded that Strauss's *Annenpolka* be played. The *Hofballmusikdirektor* did not have the music. He had to ask Strauss to 'guest conduct' the piece. Then a resourceful bureaucrat decided that Strauss might 'occasionally be asked to conduct the court ball music'. On 27 April 1854 he conducted his new waltz *Myrtenkränze (The Bride's Myrtle Wreath)* which he had composed for the wedding of the twenty-four-year-old Emperor to the sixteen-year-old Princess Élisabeth ('Sissy') of Bavaria. It was one of the last great festivities in the style of true Habsburg splendour. The city of Vienna became one large ballroom, filled with garlands, illuminations, music and people. After the bride arrived in a gilded coach drawn by eight white Lippizaner horses, the newspapers wrote that she looked like a fairytale princess. She wore a pink silk dress heavily embroidered with silver thread, crowned with a diamond diadem entwined with red and white roses.

The patriotic pieces that Strauss wrote in those years – the *Emperor Franz Josef March, Wiener Jubel-Gruss March, Viribus Unitis March, Kaiserjäger March*, among others – were a reflection of popular sentiment rather than his efforts to ingratiate himself with the Emperor. Strauss was no turncoat and certainly no sycophant. The Revolution of 1848 had had little political or social significance for him. It had been an expression of protest. As he got older, he was a *Weltbürger* – a citizen in the larger world of beautiful melodies – though he always remained a true Viennese at heart, always grateful to the influence of his native city. 'I owe the formation of my talent only to my *Vaterstadt Wien*,' he said in 1894, at the end of his life. He was Vienna's Pied Piper, with the whole population, poor and rich, barons and shopkeepers, dancing to his tune. The tune sounded of progress and change, but was not directed against the person of the Emperor whom Strauss admired throughout his life. He was probably the most popular man in Vienna, after the Emperor. The Viennese needed Strauss's waltzes as much as they then still needed the Emperor. It was said they could not live without his music; some could not even die without it.

Elisabath of Bavaria, who married the Emperor Franz Joseph in 1854.

One rich woman asked in her will be be buried to the sounds of Strauss. Not a bad idea.

On 20 July 1853 the *Theaterzeitung* reported:

Over four thousand people came to the Beer Hall last night attending the garden party for the benefit of Kapellmeister Johann Strauss. Four orchestras played alternately. At nine o'clock Strauss conducted the tone-poem *The Battle at Leipzig*, with 234 musicians. It was a great success. His newest waltz, *Knall-Kügerl*, was also enthusiastically received. The piquant melodies had to be repeated many times.

This was not merely low-brow musical sentiment. A few weeks earlier Hans von Bülow listened to a Strauss concert and said, 'His orchestra is excellent and his waltzes are very piquant.'

During the first twenty years of his public career Strauss wrote more than three hundred dances – waltzes, polkas, marches, quadrilles. He never did a sloppy job; he remained a fastidious craftsman even under pressure. He was bothered by many fears and anxieties, but he was never afraid of drying up or of running out of ideas. He could write anywhere and anytime. When he had no notepaper, he might write on the back of a menu, on his starched cuff, on a hundred-guilder note, on a handkerchief. Once he had an idea in bed and sketched the melody on the sheet. He often conceived an idea and worked it over in his head while he was being driven from one ballroom to another, like his father who wrote his *Travel Galop*, Opus 85, in a mail coach. Some great ideas came to him after a long hard night in the ballroom when he was resting for a few minutes, too tired to get up and go home. Sometimes he re-wrote a piece several times until he was satisfied that the spontaneity of the composition was not endangered by any unnecessary artifice. He sensed instinctively that it was such spontaneity which affected the people and created the real success of a piece; he knew the supreme secret of creation – simplicity. Some of his finest melodies are basically very simple. What could be more simple than the D major triad in *The Blue Danube*?

In the early morning of 14 February 1860 Strauss sat alone at a table in the Sofiensäle. He was exhausted. The guests and the musicians had gone home. All around him the charwomen were cleaning up, putting the chairs on top of the tables, getting the place ready for the next night.

At that moment a man approached Strauss. He introduced himself as a member of the committee arranging the ball of the Technical College that evening for which Strauss had contracted to compose a new waltz. The visitor asked whether he might take the new waltz home and show it to the committee. Incidentally what was the title?

Strauss shook his head. There was no title. There was no waltz. Not a single note. He had not had time to think of it even.

In later years, Strauss often told his friends the story with a touch of wistfulness. The committee man had looked so unhappy that Strauss felt really sorry for him. He reached for the first piece of paper he could find. It happened to be a soiled menu. He turned it over and on its back wrote the beginning of a new waltz. *Accelerationen*, Opus 234, which is now considered the first of his mature, great waltzes in which he found new ways and extended the form. In the first part Strauss imitates the whirring sound of the wheels – very appropriate for the students and professors of the Technical College who would dance to the music that night. He wrote other dances with 'technical' titles for the balls of the college – the *Electro-Magnetic Polka*, the *Soundwaves Waltz*, the *Fly Wheels Waltz*, the *Motors Waltz*, the *Electrophor Polka* – a long time before Prokofiev and other Russian composers wrote the sounds of wheels, steel hammers and factory noises into their scores – not always for artistic reasons.

Originally dance pieces had no special titles. When Bach wrote Allemande, Courante, a Sarabande or Gigue, he was merely indicating the musical form and also giving an indication of tempo. Similarly, Haydn, Mozart and Beethoven wrote German Dances. Only occasionally was there a reference to the dance's place of origin – Beethoven's *Mödlinger Tänze*, or Schubert's *Atzenbrugger Tänze*, for instance. Lanner and the first Strauss began giving titles to their waltzes. Publishers were all for it. They soon found out that a piece with a title that people remembered was a better seller.

The early titles were 'naturals'. Father Strauss wrote his Opus 1, *Täuberl Walzer*, for the Two Doves Inn where it was first performed. His first success, the *Kettenbrücken Waltz*, had its premiere at the Kettenbrücke Inn. Soon titles began to tell a story: Lanner wrote his *Trennungswalzer (Separation Waltz)* after he broke with Strauss, while Strauss's finest waltz, *Loreley-Rhein-Klänge* reflects the seductive song of the siren.

The younger Johann extended the idea of the title, as he extended his father's musical form. His best sound almost as beautiful as his best melodies: *Künstlerleben, An der schönen blauen Donau, Geschichten aus dem Wienerwald, Frühlingsstimmen, Freut euch des Lebens*! In his earlier years when he wrote so many dances, it was often difficult to think of a title. For the journalists he wrote *Morgenblätter (Morning Papers)*, for the students of the Medical Faculty the *Fast Pulse Waltz*, for those of the Law Faculty the *Jurists' Ball Dances*. He thought of the nations of the Habsburg Empire when he wrote a *Czech Polka*, a *Serb Polka*, a *Pester Csárdás*, a *Slav Potpourri* and a *Warsaw Polka*. For special occasions in ruling circles he wrote the *Napoleon March* (for Napoleon III), the *Coronation March* for Czar Alexander II of Russia, the *Myrtle Blossom Waltz* for the Crown

Notes made by Strauss on the programme of a Court ball of the music to be played and the times of each piece.

Anfang			Ende
8.45	1.	1ter Walzer	8.51
8.56	2.	1te Française	9.11
9.16	3.	1ter Polka tremblante	9.22
9.27	4.	2ter Walzer	9.33
9.38	5.	2te Française	9.53
10. Uhr	6.	Cotillon	11 Uhr
11.45	7.	3ter Walzer	11.50
11.54	8.	Lançe	12.14
12.18	9.	2te Polka tremblante	12.23
12.27	10.	3te Française	12.42
12.46	11.	4ter Walzer	12.51
12.55	12.	3te Polka	1 Uhr

Prince Rudolph and his wife. After the attempted assassination of the young Emperor Franz Joseph I in 1853, Strauss wrote the *Rescue-Glory March*.

Later on the greedy publishers began thinking up what they considered good titles and asked Strauss to write waltzes to fit. When Fritz Simrock in Berlin suggested *Kaiserwalzer (Emperor Waltz)* he was thinking of Kaiser Wilhelm I, but Strauss wrote it for his own Emperor. Sometimes he changed an earlier title. *Thunder and Lightning*, Opus 324, became *Shooting Stars*. But he never let the audience think up a title, as his father had once done. On 13 February 1833 Father Strauss announced at Sperl's that he had composed a new waltz, as yet untitled, and it was for the public to christen it – a good publicity stunt. Everybody was asked to write a suggestion on the back of a ticket. At midnight the new waltz, Opus 61, was performed and a pretty girl was asked to select one ticket from a large urn. The excitement turned into disappointment when the name appeared: *Tausendsapperment Walzer*. The experiment was never repeated.

Next to titles, dedications were important. People would always look at them, as they now look at the index in the memoirs of a celebrated contemporary, hoping to find themselves listed. Johann Strauss dedicated some of his finest works to the people close to him: to his wives Jetty and Adele, his friends Tilgner, Grünfeld, Brahms and Lenbach. The *Rathausball Waltz*, Opus 428, was given 'to my dear Vaterstadt Wien'. He dedicated many works to emperors, kings and other royalty, among them the Czar, the Shah of Persia, the Grand Duchess Alexandra and Austria's finance minister, Baron Carl Bruck, for the *Champagne Polka*, Opus 211. Strauss may have had his reason.

7

Josef-the most gifted Strauss

After the sudden death of his favourite brother in 1870, Johann Strauss said, 'Josef was the most gifted among the three of us. I am only the more popular one.' Strauss's admiring biographers use this quote as proof of his modesty, but it really shows his intellectual honesty and musical acumen. Posterity has confirmed his judgement.

Josef Strauss's finest waltzes have great beauty and poetic melancholy. As a composer he is closer to Schubert than to his father or brother. He was a kind-hearted, sensitive, difficult man. His gentleness made him the most vulnerable of the three brothers. From his father and grandfather he had inherited a touch of melancholia. When his father wanted him to become an officer in the regular army, Josef, then not yet twenty, wrote early in 1845, 'Please leave me where I am, and what I am. Don't take my life away from me. It could bring me many joys . . . I do not want to kill human beings. I do not want to be distinguished by a higher military rank for my services in a man hunt. I want to be useful to humans as a human, and to the state as a citizen.'

He was born on 22 August 1827, twenty-two months after Johann in the inn Zum Ritter (The Knight). He was a shy boy; he soon began writing poems that were sad and haunting: *Elegie, Der Totengräber (The Grave-Digger)*. He was a late romanticist; he also wrote drama, drew and painted. (He wrote the recitatives for Eduard Devrient's revised German translation of Gluck's *Armide*.) He did not have the easy, winning charm of his elder brother, but his melancholy eyes, dark hair and sensuous mouth made him very attractive. In some pictures he resembles the young Liszt. Yet this young romantic wanted to have a bourgeois career as an engineer. He was interested in music and played the piano well, but he certainly did not want to be a professional musician.

After leaving school he studied engineering and architecture at the Polytechnic. Somehow his mother managed to get the money out of

his father. By the time the elder Strauss died, Joef worked as a draughtsman at the office of the City Architect. He was fascinated by diagrams, not by scores. He qualified as an architect, and in 1851 designed the waterworks in Trumau. Later he became chief engineer and designer in a machine-spinning plant. His career seemed settled, and he began seriously working as an inventor, and applied for various patents. He devised a new table of logarithms for secondary schools and a street cleaning machine which was tested and bought by the Vienna City Council.

Then, one night in 1853, his brother Johann collapsed from overwork, and was ordered to rest. What was to happen to the orchestras, which supported the family? The obvious solution, proposed by Johann, and seconded by his mother: Josef would have to take over 'for a while'. He refused, gently but firmly. He had once fought it out when his father wanted him to become an officer in the army. He was not going to give in now just because the orchestras were in jeopardy. He would not do it; moreover he did not have the gift.

Johann, sick in bed, shook his head, and said, quietly but emphatically, 'You are the most gifted of us, Pepi. One day you will be a greater composer than Father or I.' Josef was too surprised to answer. He knew that Johann believed what he was saying. He was already on the defensive when he said that the very idea of performing in front of thousands of people would be a nightmare for him. He was

The Church of St Charles and the Polytechnic School where Josef studied engineering and architecture.

an introvert; he had not inherited the Strauss flair for exhibitionism. Hedging, he said, 'I couldn't replace you. I don't even play the violin.'

'It doesn't matter. You have the Strauss personality. You will conduct with the baton. Meanwhile, you'll learn to play the violin.'

There was not the slightest doubt in Johann's voice. He talked with complete conviction. Josef later admitted it was his brother's absolute confidence that had made him agree. Also, he *was* the second-eldest, and somebody had to earn money for the family. Johann had done it for quite a few years, had overdone it, and was now sick. On 21 July 1853 Josef wrote to his fiancée, Karoline Pruckmayer:

My dear Linchen – the unavoidable has happened. I'm playing today for the first time at Sperl's. Before the performance I'm rehearsing with the orchestra. I deeply regret that this had to happen so suddenly. I comfort myself that you will be thinking of me, as I think of you.

Josef's initial, instinctive fear had been justified. It wasn't only 'for a while'. He never went back to his drawing board. The Viennese waltz experts – the whole populace – observed him critically. He had none of his father's exuberance, of his brother's bewitching charm, but many women were impressed. They said Pepi was not dashing like Johann, but *very* interesting, with his sad eyes and relaxed elegance. Someone wrote that he looked like 'a dark demon'. The women said that he was fascinating; there was something enigmatic about Josef. Moreover people were moved; Johann Strauss was sick and Josef had taken over – exactly as his brother had done after the death of their father.

The critics, however, unimpressed by the emotional elements in the situation, nevertheless agreed that Josef managed the difficult meta-morphosis from dilettante to professional in an astonishingly short time. Strauss had been absolutely right about his brother's talent. Once Josef made up his mind, he applied his discipline as an engineer to the study of music. He began studying harmony and orchestration with Professor Doleschal, Strauss's former teacher. And he worked with Franz Amon who had earlier taught the violin to his older brother.

Josef was no fool. He knew that in the world's waltz capital a waltz conductor was accepted only after he had composed and successfully introduced his own compositions. It had been like that since the days of Lanner and his father. On 31 August, only five weeks after Josef's debut with the orchestra, the *Theaterzeitung* reported on the village feast in Hernals, at Unger's Casino. 'At the big ball on the 29th Josef Strauss performed his new waltz *Die Ersten und die Letzten* [*The First and the Last*]. It had to be repeated no less than six times.'

ABOVE The cover to Josef's first waltz, *The First and the Last*, which was repeated six times at its first performance.

OPPOSITE Josef's wife, Karoline, with their daughter.

The critics agreed with the audience, but it was his brother's verdict that mattered most to Josef. Back from his rest cure on 15 September, he looked at Josef's first waltz. He nodded, as to himself; he wasn't surprised at all. It was good – just as he had predicted.

Josef Strauss's music is quite different from his father's and elder brother's. They wrote mostly in major keys. Josef preferred the minor – in his music and his life. The Viennese, who instinctively sense these things, soon began calling him 'the Schubert of the dance composers'.

Josef was the only Strauss who was happily married. Karoline understood him; she knew it wasn't easy to be the wife of a Strauss in Vienna. For a while they lived at the Hirschenhaus with Anna, his mother. After their daughter was born, they moved away.

There is much warmth and poetry in Josef's music. He may have been a better musician than Johann, but he is less effective – just as one generation previously Lanner was more poetic and less effective than the first Johann Strauss. Josef did not have his brother's dionysiac sweep and spontaneity, but he had more depth. It takes longer to appreciate

his best waltzes, but they stay with you: *Dorfschwalben aus Österreich (Village Swallows from Austria)*, *Delirien (Delirium)*, *Sphärenklänge (Music of the Spheres)*, *Mein Lebenslauf is Lieb' und Lust (Live, love and laugh)*.

In spite of the title of his first waltz, *The First and the Last*, Josef soon wrote another. He called it, with disarming frankness, *The First after the Last*. It was the beginning of the most miraculous development in the Strauss dynasty. During the following seventeen years the former engineer and architect composed 222 works. The finest of them rank with the masterpieces of Johann. After the first performance of his *Delirienwalzer*, Johann happily embraced his brother and said, 'Pepi, you are a real Strauss!'

There was no jealousy between them. Josef was devoted to his elder brother. Johann loved his brother's *Schwermut*, the soft melancholy apparent in the life and work of many Austrian artists. Jetty, Strauss's first wife, understood her brother-in-law. Once she wrote to his wife, 'If Pepi had only a little of Jean's suada, he would be much better off. . . . He is too reserved, always sitting in his room. . . . He is all within himself and shuns all pretence, but today's world believes in pretence.' Yet when Josef wanted to do something, he did it. On 23 June 1856 he performed for the first time on the violin at the Zeisig. He must have been a very talented player to learn in three years what many cannot learn in six.

Unlike his father who often complained that he had to write new waltzes or his brother who could not help writing them, Josef wrote, at least in the beginning, against his will. He remains the paradox, the introvert of the Strauss family. He was so reticent that, he once said, he had not been in St Stephen's Square for a whole year. He would sit at home, working at night, smoking too much, drinking too much black coffee, sleeping too little. He never walked in the Vienna Woods, yet he instinctively, with the true poet's intuition, caught the mood of the Austrian landscape when he wrote *Village Swallows from Austria*. The waltz has the simplicity of one of Schubert's best-loved songs, *Der Lindenbaum (The Lime Tree)*. 'Who, since Schubert's death, was inspired to write such a melody?' asks H.E. Jacob. 'Josef reaches the celestial region of the Impromptus, the *Moments musicaux*. Such ideas seem to come straight from God.'

Josef Strauss's titles are often deceiving. His most popular waltz has the most misleading title of all, *Mein Lebenslauf is Lieb' und Lust* (literally *My life's course is love and pleasure*). It covers up for a life of inner tension and deep melancholy, hidden under a thin veneer of bourgeois restraint and artistic discipline. There were no affairs with admiring women. He was completely happy with Karoline and his only daughter. On Easter Sunday, 1869, he wrote from Pavlovsk to

OPPOSITE The late Biedermeier style of furnishing, shown in a watercolour by Rudolf von Alt.

his wife, 'I do not want to live separated from you anymore. Only the thought of you enables me to stay here and do my work.'

For some time Johann and Josef conducted the orchestra alternately. Each had his fans, but it was a happy competition with no hint of jealousy and intrigue. When Johann spent more time composing, Josef took charge of the organization. He would accompany his brother to Russia, and sometimes was in sole charge there. When Eduard, the third brother, joined the family business and sometimes created problems, Johann always sided with Josef. At the Hirschenhaus Anna Strauss tried to keep a semblance of harmony in the family, but she did not often succeed. The disappointment may have contributed to her end.

When she died on 23 February 1870, Josef collapsed at her bedside and had to be carried out. Afterwards he was unable to throw off a deep depression. On 17 April he gave a farewell concert in Vienna

OPPOSITE The style of Hans Makart which replaced Biedermeier and was reflected in fashions of architecture and dress.

A cartoon of the three Strauss brothers, from left to right, Josef, Johann and Eduard.

Josef was the most artistic of the brothers, and painted this watercolour of his wife Karoline.

before taking the orchestra to Warsaw where they had a contract to perform at Anton Wlodkowski's Schweizertal. Everything went wrong in Warsaw. Seven musicians did not arrive. Josef had to ask Vienna for replacements. The rehearsals did not go well. Josef had problems with his first violinist. One piece especially was not shaping well, and he decided to cut the bars that were giving difficulty. The first three concerts were without a hitch, but on the fourth night the first violinist either forgot or wanted to get even with his conductor.

He overlooked the cut; there was momentary chaos. Not many guests at Wlodkowski's had noticed the incident, but for Josef, who had been on the verge of a breakdown, it was the last straw. He collapsed on the podium, fell down four steps, and remained lying, bleeding from nose and mouth. He had suffered a severe concussion of the brain.

The musicians cabled Vienna. Josef's wife and Johann arrived at once. After a few days he recovered consciousness and was taken back to Vienna. The local papers concocted a sensational story from Warsaw. The correspondent of the *Posener Zeitung* reported that Josef Strauss was beaten up by a group of Russian officers 'because he refused to play until the early morning hours'. There was a furore in Vienna where the Russians enjoyed no sympathy. The report was completely untrue. Several intoxicated Russian officers had beaten up a concierge named Strouza. The name was confused with that of Strauss. In Vienna the denial created the opposite effect. Many people were convinced that something sinister was going on, and that the Strauss family was trying to hush it up. Soon there were other rumours. When Josef died on 22 July, it was said he had been killed in Warsaw, buried secretly and that a wax figure had been brought to Vienna for the official funeral. The macabre story was readily accepted when it became known that Josef's widow had refused to permit an autopsy request to find out the cause of Josef's frequent fainting spells and his prolonged attacks of neuralgia. A brain tumour was suspected.

Josef Strauss was forty-three when he died, one year younger than his father. His brother Johann sensed that something died with Josef that would never come back.

8
The White Nights of Pavlovsk

In the summer of 1854 Johann Strauss spent several weeks in Bad Gastein. His doctors had sent him there for the cure, and for long walks in the woods. They forbade him to do any work. Above all he must avoid worry. Strauss was a popular patient with his doctors. He was a hypochondriac, always afraid of draughts and colds. He paid his bills regularly, and he was famous. Having him as a patient increased the doctor's prestige and his fees.

In Bad Gastein, Strauss became acquainted with a gentleman from St Petersburg, who introduced himself as the new manager of the Tsarskoye Selo Railway Company. This was the first railway line in Russia, opened in 1837, from St Petersburg's Vitebsk station to Tsarskoye Selo (now known as Pushkin after the poet, who went to school there), the summer residence of Catharine II, and on to Pavlovsk. In the 1780s the Scottish architect Charles Cameron had built a palace there for Paul I, the son of Catherine. But the railway manager was more interested in the large, elegant Vauxhall restaurant near the station, financed by the railway. Popular concerts were given there each evening in summer, but recently the 'better people' in St Petersburg, the aristocrats and rich burghers, had been staying away from the Vauxhall, and the railway company was in trouble. The manager, however, had a flair for public relations. He had seen Strauss performing in Vienna, and was convinced that he was the answer to the railway's problems. He offered Strauss a contract with figures that were fantastic by contemporary standards: 20,000 roubles plus expenses for the season from the middle of May to the middle of September. After Strauss's great success the fee was increased to 40,000 roubles. Strauss signed the contract after the manager agreed that he would not have to stay at an hotel. The railway put an elegant villa surrounded by a park at his disposal.

Strauss needed the money; no one in Vienna could pay him any-

The Vauxhall restaurant, Pavlovsk, at the end of the first railway line from St Petersburg.

thing like that. He also hoped that the appointment would cause favourable comment at the court of Franz Joseph I. Czar Nicholas had given military assistance to the young Emperor in 1849 against his rebellious Hungarians. Strauss's great ambition was to be given the title *Hofballmusikdirektor*. Perhaps, after Pavlovsk. . . .

He arrived in St Petersburg in May 1855, leaving Josef in charge in Vienna. Strauss took only a few first-desk men from Vienna; the other orchestra members were to be recruited in St Petersburg, with the help of Johann Promberger, a pianist and composer who worked at the Imperial Music Academy.

The expectations of the railway manager were at once satisfied. The fame of Johann Strauss attracted members of the court, the aristocracy and the rich bourgeoisie of St Petersburg, who all took the train to Pavlovsk. Soon everybody went there who could afford it. Young Nikolai Rimsky-Korsakov went there as a youth and never forgot it. Once the Czar himself appeared at a concert and ordered his favourite piece, the *Peasants' Polka*. 'It caused more applause than a movement of a symphony by Beethoven since even the members of the orchestra

129

ПОЧЕТНЫЙ БИЛЕТЪ № 530

КОННОГВАРДЕЙСКІЙ МАНЕЖЪ

въ Понедѣльникъ 14-го Апрѣля 1886 года.

JOURNÉE DE GALA

КОНЦЕРТЪ JOHANN STRAUSS

въ пользу С.-Петербургскаго Комитета попеченія о сестрахъ

КРАСНАГО КРЕСТА

и Общества попеченія о бѣдныхъ и больныхъ дѣтяхъ.

I. Оркестръ Л.-Гв. Преображенскаго полка.
II. Симфоническій концертъ подъ упр. Проф. С.П.Б. Консерваторіи Зике.
III. Концертъ произведеній Johann Strauss подъ личнымъ его управлен.

Начало въ 1 ч. и окончаніе въ 6 ч.

Предсѣдательница Комитета
попеченія о сестрахъ Краснаго креста

А. Шуберт

Предсѣдательница Общества
попеченія о бѣдныхъ и больныхъ дѣтяхъ

Гофмейстерина Е. Нарышкина

S.106a.

joined in the applause. They forgot that the composition was really terrible trash. I don't believe it will do as much in Vienna as here,' wrote Strauss to Carl Haslinger.

The season in Pavlovsk was exhausting. There was a performance every night. 'We never go to bed before half past six in the morning. The other day it was seven o'clock, after we'd played for our pleasure Beethoven and Mozart with Promberger.' The concerts began at 7.30 p.m., and lasted until midnight. Often people asked for encores and repetitions, and the concert ended only when the bell at the nearby station announced the departure of the last train to St Petersburg. Strauss would stop in the middle of a piece, and everybody would rush for the train.

One night he conducted a new composition, the *Pavlovsk Forest Polka*, which had a terrific success. When the bell rang people stayed in their seats, cheering and demanding yet another repetition. Even the appearance of two railway employees to hurry the passengers could not break up the performance. It was July, one of the 'white nights' of Pavlovsk when the countryside is magically beautiful in the soft, silvery light of the sun, just below the horizon. No one felt like going to bed. Strauss left the platform and told the musicians to take their instruments and leave. The enthusiasm of the audience forced them to return. Suddenly there was a whistle – and then the sound of the engine. The last train had gone.

More cheers and applause. Strauss told the public, in French, that they would perform one more hour, if everybody would pay two roubles for charity. The audience happily paid up, and there were more polkas and waltzes. Afterwards everybody dispersed in the large park, waiting for the early morning train to St Petersburg. It was a mild night. No one regretted being there.

Strauss spent twelve summers in Russia. He loved his grateful audiences, although their enthusiasm was sometimes trying. After an especially successful concert he might be carried home on the shoulders of his admirers. Sometimes he escaped his fans by slipping out through a back door. According to one story he would put on a false beard to remain unrecognized.

He made influential friends. Grand Duke Constantine, a brother of the Czar, asked Strauss for permission to play the cello in the orchestra as the aristocrats in Vienna had done in the time of Beethoven. Everybody wanted to have an autographed picture of Strauss. The railway company had 100,000 printed and sold them for ten kopeks each at the stations. Strauss wrote many pieces for his appreciative audiences. Once he wrote to Haslinger, 'Herr Rather tells me that I am the only one able to write for Asia, and showed me letters from Asia. . . . You will soon get a waltz which I wrote for the

131

taste of Asia.' He composed a piano fantasy, *In a Russian Village*, and several quadrilles and polkas.

The women of St Petersburg were mad about him. His private secretary Leibrock had to answer dozens of love letters every week. Strauss was always reticent about his private life, but he needed the admiration of women – they stimulated him. Once a Russian officer came to see him and said regretfully he would have to challenge Strauss to a duel. Pistols. The officer said he was sorry but this could not go on.

'What cannot go on?' Strauss asked.

'My wife sends you red roses every day.'

Strauss asked the officer to accompany him to his villa. At the back of the house were two unfurnished rooms. They were filled with flowers.

'They've all come during the last two days,' Strauss said. The officer apologized, and they shook hands.

On his frequent visits to St Petersburg he met the daughter of a wealthy man, and was often invited to the beautiful house. According to a family story Strauss was there at lunch one day, when the girl's father got up, announced the engagement of his daughter to Strauss, and even stated the day of the wedding. It has never been quite clear how deeply Strauss was involved, but he was shocked and went to see the Austrian ambassador, Count Emmerich Széchenyi. He said he had talked to the girl, he liked her, but he had never proposed to her, and he certainly was not going to marry her. The ambassador pondered the dilemma, and said diplomatically that one must do nothing hasty.

'I suggest masterful inactivity.'

'But the wedding is announced for next week.'

'There must be no scandal now. Leave it to me.'

At this point the story becomes hard to believe. On his way to the wedding ceremony Strauss was stopped by 'two men in a troika', who took him away and brought the reluctant bridegroom to the house of the Austrian ambassador. Count Széchenyi allegedly explained to the father of the bride that there would be no wedding.

There is, however, no doubt about his love affair with Olga Smirnitzki. His letters to her exist. He met her after a concert during one of the white nights. They were walking in the park, and Strauss fell in love with this Russian girl. Some romantic biographers have compared her to the beautiful Tatjana in Pushkin's *Eugene Onegin*. 'Romantic, moving, sentimental and probably bothering him a lot,' writes H.E. Jacob. 'A creature of Pushkin . . . literature surrounded her brown locks, the white forehead . . . there was a glissando between mockery and exaltation.' All this is based on conjecture. In 1926 – many years after his death – Strauss's third wife, Adele, included

OPPOSITE The romantic scenery of Helental, near Baden, where Strauss went for his health.

OVERLEAF The second Johann Strauss conducting at a Court ball.

some of his letters to Olga in the volume *Johann Strauss Writes Letters*.
The selection was made by his widow in a rather arbitrary manner.

Adele Strauss received the letters that her husband had written to
Olga from the widow of a Russian court painter, Pauline Swertshov,
who had once been a close friend of Olga Smirnitzki. As an old lady,
she went to see Strauss's widow in Vienna, and told her about Olga.
Apparently the beautiful Russian woman survived her passion, made
a good bourgeois marriage, and had lived another twenty-six years, a
contented, perhaps resigned matron, surrounded by children and
grand-children.

In one of his letters to her Strauss writes:

My beloved child Olga, I begin to believe more and more that you are
the woman that God wanted for me. The very thought of living without
you makes my heart stop beating. Leibrock who sits next to me tries to
disturb me in my happiness. He thinks Olga is a pretty girl whom I respect
and like but do not really love. . . . How silly he is, the poor man!

Yours, JEAN

3:45 a.m. At last, Leibrock is asleep. I am glad. I kiss your heart. Please send
me a few words.

Yours, JEAN

OPPOSITE Strauss playing at the
funeral of a lady who had
requested burial to the sound of
Strauss waltzes.

137

He was thirty-three when he wrote this letter. She was just over twenty. Their relationship had to remain absolutely secret. Her family, who belonged to the upper-class bourgeoisie, had 'plans' for her. She was to marry a man with a secure State position. It had all been decided; apparently, Olga's opinion had never been asked. The correspondence between her and Strauss was carried on as between secret agents. Olga would fold her letters small and conceal them in a hole in a certain tree in the park which surrounded Strauss's villa. The faithful Leibrock would fetch them, and later bring back the answer. Strauss confessed to Olga that there was somebody in Vienna, a young woman called Elise, but if Olga would only say one word, Strauss would write to his mother, and she would straighten it out with Elise and her family 'in a sensitive and fine manner'. He

Anna Strauss in old age.

depended much on his mother, even as a grown man. It is doubtful that Olga understood. From his letters one does not get the impression that she was particularly sensitive or feminine. Once he wrote:

Even before the concert I felt, possibly without a reason, a strong melancholy that was caused by Schumann's music. Why can't I be like another man? Olga, I am very unhappy. I never cried in my life. . . . Today, I confess it to you, I did cry.

Eventually Strauss made up his mind, and went to see Olga's mother to tell her about his intentions. Her father had refused to talk to him. The meeting with Olga's mother was not pleasant, and gave him no hope. 'She was unkind and indelicate to me. She asked me to hand over your letters. I said I would take them to my grave. She told me brutally that she thought my health was not good, and *I might die any minute.*' Strauss underscored these words. 'She said that *jamais, jamais ne s'arrangera cette affaire.*' There *is* a touch of Pushkin there.

Strauss told Olga's mother that he would rather burn these letters than return them to Olga's father. 'I need these letters for my life, and cannot live without them.' Once he writes how he got a letter from her as he was on his way to a concert. He tried to read it, 'but the light was not strong enough'. He read the letter during interval, 'while all the beautiful women of St Petersburg walk by and I hear their crinolines rustling'. It is all very human, very immature and perhaps very typical of a man who was admired by women everywhere, but not understood by the girl with whom he had fallen in love, even though she was interested in music and composed a little.

Late in 1859 Strauss wrote to Olga from Vienna. He admitted that he had talked about her, and now 'all the women talk of Olga'. At a masked ball at the Redoutensaal a beautiful woman wearing a mask 'told me she would like to be Olga'. It is not surprising that Adele Strauss considered it safe, from *her* point of view, to publish these letters.

As time went on the Pushkin tragedy faded into a bittersweet Viennese operetta. In the end there are some compositions, written perhaps for Olga, and the polka-mazurka *L'Espiègle*, Opus 226, that might have been composed by Olga but was certainly revised by Strauss – and some memories. He never mentioned her in later years.

9
Number 1: Jetty

None of Strauss's three marriages was conventional. His first wife, Henriette (Jetty), had been living for almost twenty years with Moritz Todesco, a rich man who liked to be called 'Ritter von Todesco'. They had two daughters who were permitted to take the name Todesco, even though their parents were not married. Proof exists that Henriette, a singer, after 1841 had five other children by other men. It is doubtful that Strauss knew about all of them.

His second marriage was a failure almost from its beginning. Angelika Dittrich was twenty-five years younger. In the end there was a painful divorce. Strauss tried to forget this episode as quickly as he could.

And to be able to marry Adele, who was Jewish, Strauss had to leave Vienna and give up both his Austrian citizenship and membership of the Roman Catholic Church. Austria's strict marriage laws made it impossible for him to remarry in Vienna. He had to establish his legal residence in Coburg where Duke Ernst von Sachsen-Coburg-Gotha, an admirer of the composer, signed the divorce decree. Emperor Franz Joseph was not pleased, but Johann Strauss never felt bound by conventions. He was an artist, and although he was probably the most popular man in Vienna after the Emperor, he never quite belonged to the Establishment – and he knew it. '*Er ist eben ein Künstler*' – what can you expect from an artist, they would say, as though that explained everything.

Strauss met Henriette Treffz in the town house of Moritz 'Ritter von' Todesco, a member of the new Ringstrasse bourgeoisie. 'Old Vienna' had ended with the Imperial decree of 20 December 1857 which ordered that the old ramparts around the Inner City be razed. The medieval moats and ditches were filled in and replaced by a wide, horseshoe-shaped boulevard, the Ringstrasse, which surrounds the old First District. Strauss, Vienna's musical commentator, wrote the

OPPOSITE Strauss was eight years younger than his first wife, Henriette Treffz.

141

Demolirer (Demolition) Polka Française, first performed at Sperl's, on 22 November 1862. On 1 May 1865 the Emperor and the Empress were driven for the first time along the empire's new *via triumphalis*.

The Ringstrasse (which the Viennese call 'der Ring') became the pride and symbol of the imperial city of Vienna, 'the visible sign of the dignity, power and wealth of the Habsburg monarchy'. It was a project worthy of Baron Haussmann. The monarchy was already in trouble and needed a visible symbol. The Ringstrasse gave its name to a pseudo-architectural style which combined the most diversified elements, ranging from the neo-gothic City Hall to the neo-renaissance splendour of the Court Opera (now the State Opera). Only relatively few examples of pure style – such as the romanesque St Ruprecht Church, Vienna's oldest, or the lovely, gothic Sankt-Maria-am-Gestade Church – remain in the historical Inner City.

Along the Ringstrasse there are the neo-renaissance museums, the neo-hellenistic Parliament, the neo-French gothic Votive Church, the Burgtheater and the University. Yet this confusing mixture of non-styles was harmoniously fused and romantically linked by several beautifully laid-out public gardens: the Burggarten, with the statue of Mozart (by Viktor Tilgner, a close friend of Johann Strauss), and the Volksgarten that had been created on the site of a former bastion, conveniently destroyed by Napoleon. At the Colonnade of the Volksgarten the members of the Strauss dynasty had some of their great triumphs.

The Emperor arriving to open the Ringstrasse in 1865.

All along the Ringstrasse, broad and beautiful with four rows of lime trees, against the backdrop of the softly rounded hills of the Vienna Woods, the nouveaux-riches built their houses, often in ostentatious style. The Ringstrasse was status. Beyond were the former suburbs where some socially ambitious burghers hired master masons to make phoney façades in the 'old German style'. It was the era of awful imitation. One no longer spent the summer in the lovely wine villages of Grinzing and Nussdorf (now citadels of the flourishing *Heuriger* industry, with carloads of tourists getting a taste of commercialized *Gemütlichkeit*). Instead one went to the Salzkammergut or, if one could afford it, to Bad Ischl where the Emperor Franz Joseph spent almost every summer of his imperial life. Strauss and later other famous waltz and operetta composers had villas there; Ischl became the summer residence of the Viennese operetta. The bicycle became fashionable.

Surrounded by the ostentatious Ringstrasse were the lovely churches and old palaces of the historic city. It was hoped that the Ringstrasse would eventually become the bridge between the old and the new; instead it remained a permanent barrier. The newly rich lived in palatial blocks, such as the Heinrichshof, opposite the opera house – which was (and remains) the heart of the music-filled city. Nikolas Dumba, banker and industrialist who had come from faraway Macedonia, had his 'palais' on the Parkring. Unlike the old aristocratic palaces a 'palais' in Viennese parlance was a big mansion with a grandiose façade, inhabited by its owner.

The architect frequently hired was Hans Makart from Salzburg, whose name later became synonymous with *Kitsch* in the grandiose manner. He made a frieze for the dining room of the Dumba palais which his biographer, Emil Pirchan, described as being 'like a dark-glowing transparent tapestry, which at the same time shimmers and glitters in every colour, the *chiaroscuro* of the painting encompasses the entire room which has come to be a monument of the Viennese style of grand display.' Other famous Ringstrasse 'palais' were built by Baron Eduard Todesco (brother of Moritz) and Friedrich Schey, both members of this financial élite.

The Ringstrasse nouveaux riches did not conform to the usual pattern. They were anything but parvenues. On the contrary. Their salons became centres of Vienna's immensely lively political, intellectual and artistic life. They supported painters and architects, introduced gifted musicians to great conductors, and actors to the director of the court theatres. Ludwig Bösendorfer (another close friend of Strauss) whose father had founded the now famous piano factory in 1828, ran a small concert hall in Prince Liechtenstein's former riding school in Herrengasse. Its acoustics were legendary.

OPPOSITE The demolition of the old ramparts round the city in preparation for the building of the Ringstrasse.

144

At the Bösendorfersaal the partisans of Wagner won their first victories, and many great musicians performed there. Bösendorfer was always present, a famous Viennese character with stove pipe trousers and top hat.

Vienna was a stimulating place during the second half of the nineteenth century: theatres, concert halls, two opera houses and the Philharmonic, whose concerts were restricted to subscribers who had inherited their seats from inspired ancestors. The system still exists, although the rule now is that the tenure of a seat expires when the subscriber does. Years ago, when the Philharmoniker sent tickets to the subscribers by registered post – to be signed for personally by the addressee – some signatures turned out to be those of relatives and friends who claimed to have 'inherited' the seats.

Henriette Chalupetzky was born in Vienna on 1 July 1818. Her grandfather who came from Prague, and her Vienna-born father were goldsmiths and silversmiths. Her maternal grandmother was Anna Margaretha Schwan from Mannheim who became immortal in German literature when Schiller, in love with her, wrote some poems

OPPOSITE The interior of the old Burgtheater in a watercolour by Klimt.

Jetty Treffz portrayed on English sheet music.

in which he addressed her as 'Laura'. Henriette later took her mother's name, Treffz, because it sounded better for an ambitious young singer than 'Chalupetzky', and sometimes she made pretensions to nobility. On her gravestone she is styled 'Henriette Strauss geborene von Treffz'. She studied singing in Vienna with a famous professor, Gentilluomo. In Dresden she appeared with Wilhelmine Schröder-Devrient in Bellini's *I Capuletti ed I Montecchi*. In Leipzig she worked with Mendelssohn. In 1837 she became prima donna of the Kärnthnertortheater in Vienna, and appeared in the world premiere of Flotow's *Alessandro Stradella* at the Theater an der Wien. Later she toured Germany and England where she was called 'the German Queen of Song' and compared to Jenny Lind. Mendelssohn dedicated several songs to her. With great wisdom she gave up the stage while

Vienna in the 1860s.

still at the height of her fame.

In 1844 she fell in love with Moritz Todesco and went to live with him. It was a public secret in Vienna that she would have married him if he had not promised his father to remain a Jew, and civilian marriage was not permitted in Catholic Austria. It did not really matter to her: in their circles she was accepted.

Henriette – or 'Jetty' to give her pet name – had never met Strauss until she invited him to a ball at her house. He accompanied the violinist Vieuxtemps and later played his *Schallwellen (Sound Waves) Waltz*, Opus 148, on the piano. The meeting was cataclysmic for both, although neither was inexperienced nor exactly young. Jetty was almost forty-five and had lived a full life; Strauss was thirty-seven and said to have been engaged no less than thirteen times, according to

The hasty note from Strauss to
Haslinger asking him to
come to his wedding the
following morning.

gossip in Vienna. Yet for both it was love at first sight.

The Strauss–Treffz affair was the big sensation of the Vienna
season. Innumerable disappointed women who had hoped to get
Strauss, a most eligible bachelor, nevertheless admitted that Jetty
would be good for him: beautiful, cultured, sensitive, a woman of
the world, 'wise after many amorous and theatrical experiences'
(Decsey). The wedding itself was an anticlimax. On 26 August 1862,
Haslinger received a hastily written note from Strauss: 'Will you come
to my place tomorrow at seven in the morning to be my support at

the wedding, one hour later? Please answer at once.' Haslinger was among the few who had known of Strauss's intentions, and had predicted a successful marriage.

The ceremony was simple, and nobody was formally dressed. Afterwards Strauss took Jetty to the Hirschenhaus. His mother was not terribly happy; she had hoped he would marry a younger, less dominating woman than Jetty. But Anna Strauss had learned not to interfere, and she sensed that Strauss would always need somebody who would look after him – not the other way around. She kissed Jetty with a good grace, and gave her son a thick wad of notes, sixty-three thousand guilders. Her sister, Josefine Waber, in St Petersburg, had carefully put aside some of Strauss's Russian earnings before he could spend it all.

The next day, Jetty wrote to Josef Strauss who was conducting in Pavlovsk:

I am so happy and blissful to belong to my Jean whom I love with all the strength of my soul and heart. I've overcome the bitter grief I had to suffer recently, and I am now able to face the future with confidence. . . . Jean's health demands a long rest. Bathing in the ocean at the Lido will be good for him. We're going tomorrow to Venice. . . .

There had been some difficulties with Moritz Todesco, who was much older than Jetty and was said to be hurt. In the end he gave them his blessing, and made her to a certain degree financially independent. The two daughters continued to live with their father.

After their return from Venice, Jetty and Strauss moved into an apartment in Singerstrasse. Several months later Eduard, Strauss's younger brother, appeared for the first time with the Strauss orchestra, playing the harp solo in the *Colonnade Waltz*, Opus 262, under his brother's direction.

10
Eduard, a problem

Eduard Strauss was the least gifted and most problematical of the three brothers. As a composer he cannot be compared with Johann and Josef, but he survived both of them and conducted the Strauss orchestra for over thirty years until he dissolved it in 1901. Thus he is nevertheless an important part of the Strauss story. Johann's friends (and most biographers) avoided him, knowing the tension between the brothers. 'He was always a little hurt,' writes Decsey. 'He couldn't quite forgive Mozart his *Don Giovanni* and his brother Johann *The Blue Danube*.' The evidence seems to support this view of him.

Eduard was the best-looking Strauss. He too had the slightly olive, 'Moorish' skin (the Viennese called it *spaniolisch*), the dark eyes, the dapper elegance; to many women he was *'der schöne Edi'*, handsome Edi. Jacob writes, 'He was not only a conductor but also *performed* the part of a conductor.' He was one of the earliest showmen in what has become a glamorous profession. It was said that the younger Johann Strauss subconsciously imitated Emperor Franz Joseph, but that Eduard Strauss took Napoleon III as his model.

He had better nerves than his father and his brothers. As a conductor he was a martinet, and demanded strict obedience from his musicians. He could deal with ballroom managers and agents; he was tough and efficient. He kept the organization together after the sudden death of Josef – something that Johann might not have been able to do.

Eduard, the last of the Strauss children, was born on 15 March 1835, ten years after Johann. He went to good schools in Vienna, and wanted to go into the consular service to become a diplomat, the antithesis of a temperamental musician. Yet even as the head of an orchestra he remained something of a diplomat, and although authoritarian and aloof, he was better suited to deal with musicians than his sensitive brother Josef. In 1863 he married Marie Klenkhart, the daughter of a coffee-house proprietor.

OPPOSITE Eduard Strauss (seated) at Niagara Falls in 1890.

Music had never been his ambition; he said he liked to write. He was interested in classical and modern languages. But he was a Strauss and, almost automatically, studied music: theory with Gottfried Preyer and Simon Sechter, the teacher of Bruckner; the violin with the indestructible Franz Amon; and, at Johann's suggestion, the harp with Zamara and Parish-Alvars. Eduard was an excellent violinist, and when the family business expanded and Johann and Josef were unable to cope, Eduard began leading the orchestra too. He performed the waltzes of his brothers exactly as they wanted them played, and is an important link in the Viennese tradition of performing Strauss.

On 5 February 1859 the papers announced 'Three Balls in One Night' at the Sofien-Bad. Three large orchestras played alternately, each under one of the Strauss brothers. In the final *Herausschmeisser-Galopp (Kick-them-out Galop)* the three orchestras played together. The three brothers also collaborated in the composition of the *Trifolien Waltz* and the *Schützen Quadrille*.

As conductor of the Strauss Orchestra, Eduard felt obliged to compose and perform his own music, but his compositions are minor compared with the work of his father and brothers, and he knew it. All his adult life he suffered from an inferiority complex. Occasionally he made trouble for his brothers. Once, when his brothers were in Russia, he decided to take the orchestra on tour without consulting them. Josef wrote to his wife that this might create serious problems

The *Trifolien Waltzer* in which the brothers collaborated.

with their publisher Sima. Unless Anna Strauss undertook to talk him
out of it, Josef threatened to move out of the Hirschenhaus.

Johann, too, needed much patience dealing with his youngest
brother. In 1892, after reading some gossip in the papers about a
'fight' with his brother, Johann wrote:

> You are mistaken if you believe what you read in the papers. . . . You are
> always suspicious. You always think I'm trying to do something mean to
> you. Can't you stop acting like that? How old will you have to be to realize
> that you must not see an enemy in your brother? . . . Sometimes our rela-
> tionship has been seriously disturbed by your ambitions, but you should
> know that my brotherly feelings have never been changed. . . . *Au fond du
> cœur* I've always remained the same *vis-à-vis* you.

Occasionally Johann gave Eduard some advice in musical matters,
although he was never sure how his brother would take it. After the
concert at the Musikverein Hall for Strauss's fiftieth year jubilee he
wrote to Eduard on 17 October 1894, 'Your orchestra played
magnificently last Sunday. Only the trumpets were not completely in
tune.' Another time he asked Eduard that his waltzes should be
played 'never too fast'. Good conductors of Strauss music still
remember this bit of advice.

Eduard was vain, always interested in titles and decorations. When
he was appointed court conductor by the Brazilian government,
he had special visiting cards printed. Johann was amused. 'One must
be careful not to irritate the Brazilian Hofkapellmeister,' he wrote to
Adele. 'That could have terrible consequences.' In a more serious vein
he said to his brother in a letter, 'A good musical idea is worth much
more than a decoration. What good is a star on my chest if my next
operetta is a failure?' Even so Johann himself accumulated quite a
collection of decorations: the Knight's Cross of the Franz Joseph
Order, the Commander's Cross of the Spanish Order of Isabella, the
Knight's Cross of the French Légion d'Honneur, the Persian Sun and
Lion Order (Fourth Class), the Russian Great Gold Medal with the
Alexander Nevsky ribbon – and a dozen others.

Eduard, however, was not the only one who cared about such
things. In 1872 Josef Ritter von Scherer, the stepfather of Jetty
Strauss, 'adopted' his son-in-law, then forty-seven, and petitioned the
Emperor – through channels, to be sure – that his title might be
inherited by his adopted son. The petition, of 14 May 1872, was signed
by Von Scherer and Strauss. One may safely assume that Jetty Strauss
was behind that move. She would have loved to be a member even of
the lower nobility. The petition was supported by the governor of
Lower Austria, but Emperor Franz Joseph I turned it down. 'His
Apostolic Majesty has awarded Strauss several citations,' writes

The front cover of Eduard's
triumphal march dedicated to
Don Pedro of Brazil.

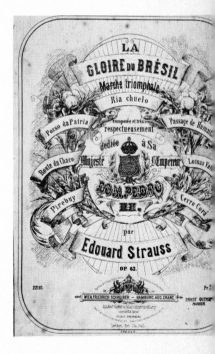

Eduard Strauss wearing all his medals, of which he was very proud.

Freiherr Lasser von Zollheim, the Minister of the Interior. 'He was named Imperial and Royal *Hofballmusikdirektor*. He received the Gold Medal for Art and Science. . . . New achievements that would entitle him to a further act of his Most Excellent Majesty are not proven.' The Emperor's decision of 9 March 1873 was a sad day for Jetty. Strauss, however, did not seem to care, and the following year *Die Fledermaus* brought him more glory than a title.

Eduard Strauss's best-known work is his *Memoirs* published in 1906, when he was seventy-one and Johann had been dead for seven years. Eduard did not write well, nor had he mellowed with age, and the *Memoirs* created much talk and misunderstanding. 'He had no sense of humour, and never got rid of his Johann complex,' wrote Decsey.

In the foreword Eduard attacks his father's biographers. 'Those who wrote about my father's life were never his friends.' He never even tried to understand why his father spent his last years with Emilie Trambusch, 'that person . . . who eventually stole the lanterns from the last resting place of "her friend"'. Johann and Josef do not come alive in the *Memoirs*. In fact they are rarely mentioned, and their genius is never acknowledged. Instead Eduard plays up his own considerable contribution to the family enterprise. 'During the *Fasching*, I employed up to 130 musicians. In one evening, after starting at 8.30 at Dommayer's, I would be at 10 at Schwender's Colosseum, at 11 o'clock in the Blumensaal, as 12.30 at the Sofiensäle . . . an enormous physical effort.' He reports, with pardonable pride, that in 1872 he was appointed *Hofballmusikdirektor*. And he is justly pleased when he says, 'I first performed Siegfried's *Funeral March* from *Götterdämmerung*, and the *Prelude* and the *Good Friday Music* from *Parisfal* in Vienna.'

A good observer, he recalls amusingly his English tour in 1885 when 'nine thousand people' came to hear him and his orchestra at the Albert Hall, where 'dukes and duchesses, lords and ladies had to fight for seats with the rest of the public.' He remembers a command performance at Windsor Castle before Queen Victoria. The programme was compiled by Princess Beatrix: Liszt's Second Rhapsody, Eduard Strauss's arrangements of pieces by Schubert, Mendelssohn, Tchaikovsky, 'a *polka française* by myself', *God Save the Queen* and the Austrian Hymn. The concert began at ten in the evening and lasted

ABOVE The certificate of Eduard's appointment as *Hofballmusikdirektor*.

Eduard conducting at a promenade concert in the Volksgarten.

The programme of Eduard's last concert in America.

three hours, but the Queen, then seventy-four, was not tired. At the end she thanked Eduard, and told him how well she remembered his father who had played at her Coronation Ball forty-eight years previously.

Eduard Strauss was happy with England, although not always so with English cooking. 'It occurred to me how well one dined with the Queen, the diplomatic corps, the Rothschilds etc., and how badly in the hotels of London. During two months we performed for three -and a half million people. . . . That can happen only in England. What I liked about the English public was not only the terrific attendance but also people's fine understanding for good music. The English love Beethoven, Schubert, Meyerbeer and Mendelssohn. Such works are mostly unknown in Vienna, where only the violin concerto is performed of Mendelssohn's works. . . . After returning to Vienna I felt painfully the difference between the warm sensitivity of the people in London and the bad taste of the Viennese.'

In March 1890 he went to America on the Bremer Lloyd steamer S.S. *Werra*, with an orchestra of forty-two and three servants. Between May and December they performed in seventy-seven cities. 'The most music-loving city on earth is Boston. . . . The most difficult concert was in Madison Square Garden in New York where the people didn't hear us well.' Many unpleasant things happened. In New York he had a sunstroke. In Omaha, Nebraska, his butler ran away in full livery 'because he didn't want to return to his wife in Vienna'. Eduard noted that 'for 50 cents a worker may buy so much meat that he, his wife and his child may eat meat four times a day'. Those were the days. He concludes that 'One can get rich faster in America but the physical exertion is much worse.'

The *Memoirs* give an exact report on a personal tragedy which had created much gossip in Vienna in 1897 and much depressed the younger Johann Strauss two years before his death. While Eduard had been travelling, his sons had made some foolish investments. His wife, without asking, had given them most of his money. 'In three years and three months my sons spent a capital of 738,600 crowns,' he wrote, and at an age when many men think of retiring, Eduard had to start all over again. On 28 November he gave a benefit concert at the Musikverein. Johann conducted his new waltz *An der Elbe*, Opus 477.

The most mysterious paragraph in the *Memoirs* says, 'Between myself and my brother Josef an agreement had been concluded in 1869 that the survivor would destroy all arrangements made by the others.' It is a statement which has puzzled all Strauss biographers. Eduard kept the agreement, which was presumably concluded to prevent other musicians from using their musical arrangements. In 1906 – the year when the *Memoirs* were published – he had several crates of musical material taken to a stove factory and burned. Many experts believe that the crates contained not only orchestral arrangements made by the brothers but also invaluable autographs and manuscripts of Johann and Josef – depriving the musical world of treasures that can never be replaced.

Eduard Strauss died in 1916. He had two sons, Johann III (1866–1939) and Josef (1868–1940). In the Strauss family all the sons are now called either Johann or Josef or Eduard; tradition remains strong, and so is the tendency towards music though the family has produced no new genius yet. Johann III took over the court music after his father's retirement, but was never appointed *Hofballmusikdirektor*. He later went to Berlin where he died. The musical tradition continues with Eduard Strauss, born in 1910, the grandchild of the younger Josef. In 1949 – one hundred years after the death of Johann Strauss I – the younger Eduard became a conductor and a specialist in Strauss music. His son, Eduard III (born 1955), and Johann IV (born 1924), another great-grandchild of Eduard, represent the present (eighth) generation. Richard Strauss and Oscar Straus, incidentally, were entirely unrelated to the Viennese family.

Eduard, Johann and Joseph Strauss.

ABOVE The front cover of *The Blue Danube*.

LEFT The notice to Johann Strauss of his appointment as *Hofballmusikdirektor*.

11

The Blue Danube

Johann Strauss and his first wife Jetty spent the summer of 1863 in Pavlovsk, while Eduard was conducting the Strauss Orchestra in Vienna. 'Eduard seems to do his job very well,' Strauss wrote to Haslinger. He also announced a *Liedl* (small song) 'in the style of Verdi . . . of which I am rather ashamed'. He had composed it for Jetty, who occasionally sang at Russian court concerts. The correspondence between Strauss and Haslinger became concerned with money matters. Strauss felt that his publisher was taking advantage of him. Once he fumed:

Your infamy is really too impertinent. In Vienna I had to give to my friend Carl Haslinger 800 Austrian florins for 400 roubles, to be paid to me in St Petersburg. Now the swine Buttner deducts the money from my salary because 'I didn't give to Carl Haslinger the equivalent of 400 roubles.' I am curious how many times you're going to deduct these 400 roubles. No joke – they cost me here 1050 Austrian florins.

Early in 1864 Jetty informed 'dear friend Haslinger' that her husband had just received his decree appointing him Imperial and Royal *Hofballmusikdirektor*. She wanted Haslinger to be the first to know 'because I am convinced that you are deeply interested in Jean's good fortune'. But relations were already strained, and a few months later they were broken. In May the *Morgenblätter Waltz (Morning Papers)*, Opus 279, was published by Strauss's new publisher, C.A.Spina.

Morgenblätter had been written during the *Fasching* of 1862. The Concordia Journalists' and Writers' Association had asked both Offenbach (who happened to be in Vienna) and Strauss to write new waltzes for their annual ball. Offenbach had a great success with his *Abendblätter (Evening Papers)*. He was all the rage, and the Viennese were as mad about him as they had once been about Rossini and the Italians.

The entrance to the Strauss villa in Maxingstrasse.

OPPOSITE Henriette Treffz.

Conversely, the Strauss waltz was not appreciated, and its composer was depressed. Today the Offenbach waltz is forgotten, but *Morgen-blätter* remains one of Johann Strauss's most popular waltzes.

On 4 December a benefit concert was announced at the Volksgarten for Josef and Eduard Strauss. '*Hofballmusikdirektor* Johann Strauss will also perform. Twenty years ago he made his debut at Dommayer's Casino with his waltz *Sinngedichte*.' The following year, Eduard substituted for his brothers in Pavlovsk, and did so well that Johann gave up regular conducting; only on special occasions would he appear on the platform.

In 1869 he bought a lovely two-storey villa in Hetzendorferstrasse 18 (now Maxingstrasse) in Hietzing, near Dommayer's. It had a yellow façade, green shutters, a gilded fence, and the windows looked out on the wall dividing Hietzing from the imperial palace of Schönbrunn.

Jetty wrote to a friend, 'The house is so nice and comfortable that we believe ourselves to be in our beloved England . . . the interior decorations are most lovely. Life in London pleased Johann so much that he didn't give in until he could call this house his own.' Jetty put in dark-red tapestries, beautiful furniture, paintings and also laurel wreaths and other symbols of fame. Strauss excused them to visitors by saying, 'My dear wife likes them . . .', but he did too. He was happy with Jetty who gave him warmth and affection. She understood people. And she knew that Strauss needed peace and time to create. She made him devote himself to composing. The daily grind of conducting the orchestras was left to Josef and Eduard. Sometimes Johann Strauss saw no dancing for months on end.

In the ten years after 1860 Johann Strauss created his greatest waltzes. He no longer thought of them primarily as dances, but as concert pieces. During these years his marriage was a happy one. Once Jetty wrote:

. . . As far as our life is concerned it is always the same – happy and intimate, based on feeling and mutual respect. My Jean is the best, most noble-minded man on earth. His heart is a treasure. I thank the Good Lord every day that he gave me this rascal who made life again desirable for me. . . .

Four years after this letter, Strauss wrote his most famous waltz. Not for orchestra, but for the Vienna Men's Choral Society. In Berlin Karl Friedrich Zelter, a close friend of Goethe, had founded the Singakademie in 1808, and soon many German cities had a men's choir. In Vienna, however, Metternich's police were suspicious about men meeting in groups. They might pretend they met to sing when they were really conspiring. When the Men's Choral Society was at last founded in 1843, Metternich told the police to keep watch over 'this poison from Germany'. In 1856 Johann Herbeck, the conductor who later became director of the Court Opera, was made chorus

master of the society and at once reformed its bad programme. It was he who conducted the first performance of Schubert's *Unfinished Symphony* in 1865, thirty-seven years after his death.

Two years later Herbeck asked Strauss to write a waltz for the *Fasching* concert of the choral society. Vienna was slowly recovering from defeat at the hands of Prussia at Königgrätz the previous year. The mood in the waltz city was subdued. Strauss told Herbeck it was the wrong moment. Moreover, he had never written a waltz for voices. Herbeck said it was exactly the moment to give people a sense of hope again, besides, Strauss could do anything if he wanted. The two men admired each other. Strauss said he had no text. Never mind, said Herbeck, he would take care of that later.

Strauss had a title, however. He remembered a poem by Karl Isidor Beck, a socially conscious poet of the pre-March era. Karl Gutzkow once called Beck 'the German Byron'. Beck had written a love poem to Vienna, or perhaps to a woman in Vienna that ended with the words '*an der Donau, an der schönen, blauen Donau*'. Strauss had lived many years in the Leopoldstadt, not far from the Danube; he knew the river was greenish or grey, and sometimes silvery, under the light of the moon – never blue. Yet the poet's imagination caught the musician's imagination. Strauss had a wonderful idea: a thirty-two-bar melody based on a single motive, the D major triad.

The Blue Danube, Opus 314, has been analysed *ad absurdum*. There

OPPOSITE An oil painting of the second Johann Strauss by Eisenmenger.

The opening bars of *The Blue Danube* in Strauss's handwriting.

has been much speculation about the impressionistic tremolo introduction of the strings. It is 'the sound of the river, known to every
swimmer'? (Jacob). Strauss gave no hint: he never talked about his
works, and did not encourage analysis. When somebody told him it
sounded like the beginning of the *Lohengrin* Prelude, he gave a shrug.
The Blue Danube is not programme music, such as Siegfried's *Rhine
Journey* or Smetana's *Vltava*. Strauss may have intended to evoke the
mood of the Danube, but for the world he had epitomized the very
mood and heartbeat of Vienna. The perpetual appeal of this waltz is
due to its identification with all that is Viennese, and it is a fact that
expatriates of that city – even though they have no real reason to feel
nostalgic – often have moist eyes when they hear *The Blue Danube*. It
is never sentimental; it has genuine sentiment.

Hanslick who often said the right thing (and sometimes the wrong)
called *The Blue Danube* 'A patriotic folk-song, without words. Next to
Haydn's *Imperial Hymn* we now have a popular hymn that sings the
glory of our country and nation. Wherever Austrians meet abroad,
the "peace *Marseillaise*" without words will be their secret mark of
identification', and he told Strauss, 'Your melody has become a
quotation.'

Like many things created in Vienna the great waltz has a history
which is somewhat ironic. Strauss gave the score to Herbeck who
assigned it to Joseph Weyl, the choral society's 'house poet', to write
the text. Weyl, a police official by profession, divided the chorus into
two half choruses who would ask each other,

> 'Wiener, seid froh!'
> 'Oho! Wieso?'
> 'Ein Schimmer des Lichts –'
> 'Wir seh'n noch nichts!'
> 'Der Fasching ist da.'
> 'Ah so, na na.'

Freely translated: 'Viennese, be glad.' 'Oho, why so?' 'A shimmer
of light –' 'We see nothing as yet.' '*Fasching* is here.' 'Oh, yes – well
then.' It sounded perhaps a little less silly when sung by the alternating
voices of the tenors and basses, but the members of the choir, solid
citizens with healthy voices, almost staged a revolt. They said the
text was just too idiotic, 'unsingable and unmelodious'. Charitable
biographers have tried to explain away the nonsense. Weyl, according
to Jacob, 'was still affected by the pre-March spirit when one could
say in lyrics what one couldn't possibly write in an editorial'. Perhaps
Weyl was referring to the depressed mood in Vienna after the lost
war, and was trying to paint the proverbial silver lining on the
horizon. But perhaps never has a beautiful melody been matched with

such a stupid text. Herbeck and Nikolaus Dumba, the rich financier in his Ringstrasse mansion who generously supported the choir, had a hard time to tell the members that they were right, the text was no good, but Strauss must not be told. They did not bother to tell the people that the message was not wrong after all. Austria was finished as a nineteenth-century superpower, and things were pretty desperate, but this was *Fasching*, so 'Viennese, be merry and gay!' The Viennese, trained by centuries of adversity, would well understand the message.

On 13 February 1867 the Men's Choral Society, conducted by Rudolf Weinwurm, presented *The Blue Danube*, accompanied by the orchestras of Josef and Eduard Strauss. It was not exactly a failure, but neither was it a resounding success. The piece was repeated only once – pretty bad by Strauss standards. He accepted the public verdict with the philosophy he often showed in bad moments: 'The waltz was probably not catching enough', he said to his friend Ignaz Schnitzer. 'But when one composes for voices one cannot think only of dancing.' To his brother Josef he said, 'I don't really care so much about the waltz but I'm sorry about the coda. It deserved success.' Many great composers have since admired the bittersweet reflection of this short epilogue.

Six months after the failure of *The Blue Danube* in Vienna the publisher Spina had hundreds of thousands of copies shipped all over the world. (Spina made a fortune on *The Blue Danube*. Strauss received only a hundred and fifty guilders for it.) At that time the average musical composition was printed from copper plates. One plate sufficed for 10,000 copies. Of *The Blue Danube*, over a hundred plates were made. The waltz had become a *succès fou* in Paris.

At the Paris World Fair in the summer of 1867 the Second Empire took a last, narcissistic view of itself. In Vienna the Ringstrasse had been built while deep cracks were already appearing in the foundations of the Habsburg Empire. The Paris exhibition, which Hans Christian Andersen called 'a Babel, a wonder of the world', opened at a time when the regime of Napoleon III was becoming shaky. Austria had an able ambassador in Paris – Prince Richard Metternich, the liberal son of a tyrannical father – who well understood that France and Austria would have to become allies, now that Prussia was getting more powerful. Metternich's wife, Pauline, born as the daughter of a Hungarian horse-racing enthusiast, was a brilliant, ambitious woman. Some called her *la grande dame* of the Second Empire. Others thought she was terrible and shocking, with her manners, affairs and excesses.

The government in Vienna allotted the immense sum of 165,000 francs for the Metternichs to give a gala party in May 1867. The Paris correspondent of the *Daily Telegraph* wrote:

A salon in Paris during the Second Empire.

OPPOSITE The front page of *Le Drôlatique* in 1867.

It is by no means easy to entertain two thousand persons, including an emperor, an empress, an Imperial prince, a king, two queens, two royal princes, grand duchesses, highnesses and all the diplomacy, wit, beauty and fashion of a great city. Yet that was what was not only attempted but thoroughly effected on Friday...

and he went on raving about

... the beds of flowers and a glittering fountain; on either side galleries lined with flowers; and to this a group of the best-looking and best-dressed people in Paris and you may have a faint idea of the beauty of the scene. ...

Strauss had been invited to Paris by Count Osmond, who had long admired his music. He was to appear with the famous Bilse Orchestra from Berlin, alternating with its permanent conductor Benjamin Bilse. He conducted at the Cercle International, but the concerts were not a success: too much was going on everywhere else. He also conducted at an Austrian Embassy ball. Even there he created no sensation, and he thought of going back to Vienna.

168

Nº 13.

DIX CENTIMES

Samedi 6 Juillet 1867.

BEAUX-ARTS
LITTÉRATURE
THÉATRES. — MUSIQUE

RÉDACTEUR EN CHEF
ALFRED DE CASTON

BUREAUX :
7, rue Saint Marc, 7

LE
DROLATIQUE
REVUE HUMOURISTIQUE ILLUSTRÉE

BEAUX-ART
LITTÉRATURE
THÉATRES. — MUSIQUE

ADMINISTRATEUR-DIRECTEUR :
V. LEBLANC

BUREAUX :
7, rue Saint Marc, 7

JOHANN STRAUSS, PAR DURANDEAU.

LES CONCERTS DU CERCLE INTERNATIONAL

One night, however, Jean Hippolyte de Villemessant, owner of *Le Figaro*, attended one of the concerts at the Cercle International, was immediately captivated by Strauss waltzes, and decided to launch their composer. Villemessant was called 'more powerful in Paris than Napoleon and Metternich together'. *Le Figaro* was not exactly pro-Napoleon, but Villemessant agreed with Metternich that a rapprochement between France and Austria against Prussia was absolutely necessary. The Prussians had significantly exhibited a big new Krupp cannon at the World Fair.

Villemessant thought Strauss would be the ideal catalyst. And, moreover, it was amusing to see a Prussian orchestra under the most Viennese of all musicians. The publisher discussed the matter with Wolff, Jouvin, Villemot and other members of his staff, who agreed. The next morning *Le Figaro* began its Strauss campaign. It was noticed that Strauss was in every way an *homme du monde* who spoke perfect French and had aristocratic manners. He was invited to the editorial offices of *Le Figaro*. He met Flaubert, Dumas fils, Théophile Gautier, Turgenev, Rochefort. Lunch was a great success. Ambroise Thomas, then very famous following the recent success of his opera *Mignon*, had a long talk with Strauss. A few days later Strauss gave a dinner for the staff of *Le Figaro*, and conducted the *Figaro Polka*, Opus 320, especially composed for the occasion. Afterwards Strauss conducted his almost forgotten waltz – *Le beau Danube bleu*, as the French called it.

The success was sensational. Brilliant French critics called it 'the waltz of waltzes', showing greater perception than their colleagues in Vienna, and Jules Barbier, librettist of Offenbach's *Tales of Hoffmann*, wrote a French text for *The Blue Danube*,

> 'Fleuve d'azur
> Sur ton flot pur
> Glisse la voile
> Comme une étoile'

The Blue Danube had at last achieved fame. *Le Journal* printed a picture series, *Le beau Danube bleu*. *Le Drôlatique* published a cartoon of Strauss by Durandeau. Strauss's wife wrote to a friend, 'Jean admits that nowhere, neither in Vienna or St Petersburg, where he had his greatest triumphs, has he had such a colossal success. . . . The French women who are crazy about Jean never try to go beyond applause. Not as in Russia where Jean got lots of love letters every day.'

The Blue Danube echo reached all the way to London. Strauss had an invitation from the Prince of Wales. Between 16 August and 25 October he gave a series of concerts at Covent Garden. *The Times* wrote:

OPPOSITE Strauss on the platform during a masked ball at the Paris Opera.

Herr Strauss, who strongly resembles his father in manner, seems also to possess a large share of those qualities which led to his father's renown. He conducts the orchestra like his father, fiddle in hand, and joins in the passages of some importance. This he does with wonderful animation. . . . The future success of the Covent Garden concerts depends materially on him.

The London premiere of *The Blue Danube* took place on 18 September. Father Strauss had written his *London Season Waltz*. The son wrote *Memories of Covent Garden*. 'Adieu, geliebtes England', he said when he left.

In Vienna Hanslick wrote of 'the fatigue and over-saturation' in the work of Strauss. The allegedly fatigued Strauss wrote his next opus, *Tales from the Vienna Woods*, perhaps even finer music than *The Blue Danube*. Having caught the likeness of the Danube in music, he now sought to portray the lovely woods that enchanted Beethoven, Schubert and many other composers. He had done the impossible when he painted the Danube blue and made it Vienna's musical consciousness. Now he expressed the traditional Viennese longing for the simple pleasures of Nature – the trees, the brooks, the flowers and the meadows. *Tales from the Vienna Woods* is a very modern waltz, the city dweller's secret longings for all the things he lacks in the grey, dark streets. The Viennese are to this day still enthusiastic nature lovers. No other big city is blessed by such a lovely diadem of wooded hills within easy reach.

172

ABOVE The sheet music of
Tales from the Vienna Woods.

RIGHT An outing into the
countryside near Baden.

It is not generally known that the first part of this waltz, with its melodic line of forty-four bars, belongs to the longest melodic ideas in music. The melody is supported by a masterful instrumentation. One does not have to see the Vienna Woods to know what they are like, for Strauss has written what is in effect a tone poem. He understood what Liszt had meant when he wrote, 'The musician who is inspired by Nature exhales in sound Nature's most tender secrets without copying them. He thinks, he feels, he speaks through Nature.' *The Blue Danube* and *Tales from the Vienna Woods* remain among Nature's most tender secrets.

'Strauss never wrote a single note that the Viennese didn't understand but he always had style and taste,' wrote Decsey. 'He never identified with the narrow-minded, uncultured *Kleinbürger* [small townsman] who confuses ecstasy with drunkenness.' Strauss understood human beings, their hidden joys and sorrows; he was able to translate their most intimate emotions into melody. This is the secret of his universal, timeless success: he is understood everywhere. Fifty years after his debut at Dommayer's Strauss admitted that he owed his talent, 'if I have some', to his native city, 'where the sounds are in the air that I heard in my ears, took in with my heart, and wrote down with my hand'. No one has explained it more clearly.

In his earlier works, until 1860, Johann Strauss, still under the influence of his father, reflected the Biedermeier atmosphere of 'Old Vienna'. One also hears an echo of the ländlers of Haydn, Mozart, Schubert and Lanner. But when the older Strauss wrote his masterpiece, *Loreley-Rhein-Klänge*, extending the waltz form from eight to sixteen bars, writing longer melodic lines, a romantic introduction and a beautiful coda, the composer became a poet. The son learned his lesson. He modelled his great waltzes after 1860 on his father's greatest waltz, probably unintentionally and subconsciously. He was more gifted and musically better educated than his father; he had better ideas and knew more about composition. And he always learned by experience, always tried to write better. His librettist Genée once recalled how carefully, almost mathematically, Strauss would count the groups of bars, designing his waltz themes, the contrasting rhythms, and working hard on the conclusions that often make or break a dance piece. The facility is deceiving, the mark of the true master. The inspiration was always there but also the cool, analytical mind. Strauss understood that melody is synonymous with music. In his greatest waltzes one sometimes seems to sense that quality of cantilena of his great Italian contemporary, Verdi.

After 1870 Strauss wrote dance music only for special occasions. Both his mother and his brother Josef – he loved them both – died in 1870. A few weeks before his mother's death he wrote one of his last great 'Dionysiac' waltzes, *Freut euch des Lebens! (Enjoy Life!)*, first performed on 15 January 1870 at the opening of the Musikverein Building, and the waltz *Neu Wien*, Opus 342, his comment on 'New Vienna'. Afterwards he was no longer just a waltz composer. True, he wrote some beautiful dances in his operettas, and he wrote some for special reasons. The *Adelenwalzer*, Opus 424, for his third wife; the *Emperor Waltz*, Opus 437, a great masterpiece, his tribute to the Emperor, and his poetic prediction of the end of an era, *Seid umschlungen, Millionen*, Opus 443, from Schiller's *Ode to Joy* which Beethoven used at the end of his Ninth Symphony. Strauss dedicated this waltz to Brahms.

When Strauss expanded the symphonic features of his concert waltzes, Hanslick accused him of 'flirting with the muses of Weimar'. The reference was to Liszt, much admired by Strauss. He sensed in Liszt's harmony and orchestration the beginning of a new musical era. He often performed Liszt's symphonic poems, although no one else in Vienna dared to. The powerful Hanslick had no love for Wagner's father-in-law, and he criticized Strauss's 'stilted themes combining endless periods and highly sophisticated harmonies . . . that irritate both ear and foot'. Strauss's 'miserable chord progressions tossed about by the trombones which might be suitable in an operatic finale full of blood and thunder, but are terrible in a waltz.'

Paradoxically the very features that irritated Hanslick, and perhaps many dancers (when he upset the one-two-three pattern by asymmetrical rhythms) today give Strauss's best waltzes the touch of genius: the 'endless periods', the 'highly sophisticated harmonies' (he often uses wind and percussion instruments, soft brass, brilliant woodwind passages), the 'miserable chord progressions'.

Strauss achieved what 'all subsequent operetta composers could not understand, the dramatic in the dance', writes Paul Henry Lang. And Mosco Carner praises 'the rich variety in the waltz . . . sensuous and languishing tunes; gay, capricious and saucy tunes which electrify both ear and foot. It is, in short, Viennese music *par excellence*, far more refined and polished than Lanner's and his [Strauss's] father's, and lit up by the spark of a great genius.'

12

Ordeal in Boston

Four years prior to the centenary celebrations of America's independence, Boston – 'the country's oldest music city' – had its own World Peace Jubilee, from 17 June to 4 July 1872. The city fathers, aware of the heroic role of the State of Massachusetts and the historical significance of the Boston Tea Party, decided that a monster concert festival, the more the merrier, would be the effective commemoration, though perhaps not completely appropriate to the style of Boston. The city was justly proud of its musical establishment. Karl Zerrahn from Mecklenburg conducted the local Handel and Haydn Society. Kapellmeister Julius Eichberg from Düsseldorf was in charge of the Museum Concerts. The committee invited some celebrities from Europe: the popular composer Franz Abt, the conductor Hans von Bülow. And Johann Strauss.

Strauss was flattered – and all set to turn down the invitation. He was afraid to travel. It was an effort to go to the Semmering, one hour away; now they wanted him to go to America.

The temptation was considerable, since the Bostonians were offering Strauss $100,000 ('the largest sum offered to any artist since the publisher Cotta paid Goethe 300,000 taler,' writes H.E. Jacob) and all expenses for himself, his wife, his valet and a chambermaid. The entire amount was to be deposited in advance at the Anglo-Bank in Vienna. Even today it would be a tempting offer. In 1872 there was not much income tax. One hundred thousand gold dollars was literally a fortune.

It was his wife Jetty who made the decision. She said that there was the money, and also the publicity and fame; that if Bülow had gone there, why not Strauss? At last he gave in. A few weeks earlier, in March 1872, Eduard had also been named *Hofballmusikdirektor*. He would keep the business in Strauss's absence. Strauss went to see his lawyer and made a will, 'May 29, 1872, before starting the journey for America. My last will!' He made Jetty his sole heir.

They left Bremen on 1 June on a small 5,000-ton liner of the North German Lloyd. The cabins were small, the berths were narrow. Even in good weather, the 'fiddles' round the edges of the tables were in use to stop things rolling off. By today's standards it was certainly not a comfortable trip.

A Prussian Guard Band happened to be aboard. They were going to tour America. They played Strauss's waltzes. Strauss would listen, smoking his cigar and drinking champagne 'as a precaution against getting seasick'. Even today many people consider champagne a sure remedy. Strauss did not dance, and told his valet Stephan to do so with all ladies aboard. They arrived in New York after fifteen days, on 16 June, and went straight to Boston.

The first thing Strauss noticed were enormous posters showing him as a 'waltz king' sitting atop a globe, holding a conductor's baton in the manner of a sceptre. Although he was amused at first, he soon became upset when he realized what he was up against. An enormous hall had been constructed in the Back Bay district for the festival. It had a platform for twenty thousand performers and an auditorium

The passenger list of the Donau in July 1872.

ABOVE LEFT An American sheet music cover depicting Johann Strauss.

with raked seating for over a hundred thousand listeners. The roof was supported by four avenues of pillars hung with flags. At the back of the stage there was a vast organ. Such was the monstrous building where he would have to conduct fourteen concerts.

The enthusiasm of the American audiences equalled the measurements of the concert hall. Strauss had been through hectic moments in Vienna, St Petersburg and Paris, but never through anything like this. Wherever he went, he was surrounded by people who tried to touch him, cheered him or wanted his autograph. At his residence he was besieged by swooning women wanting a lock of his hair as a souvenir. Stephan, the resourceful valet, found a solution: he sold clippings from a black Newfoundland dog as genuine Strauss hair. Strauss's consternation grew when he had a rehearsal. He could hear nothing but jumbled noise. No one had bothered about acoustics. It was terrifying. Fortunately Von Bülow, who was still there, assured him that he had survived the hall. Strauss later admitted that, but for Bülow's support, he might have broken his contract and run away.

The enormous hall was crowded on the evening of Strauss's first appearance. His head was spinning. The whole day had been an uninterrupted sequence of ceremonies and speeches. The atmosphere was chaotic. On the way to the platform he was preceded by six tall policemen who tried to make a narrow lane through the delirious crowds. It was noted that he was 'pale with excitement'. Behind him Stefan ceremoniously carried his violin. As he reached the centre of the platform 'a thunderous ovation went up from one hundred thousand throats'.

Round him was a veritable army of instrumentalists and singers, twenty thousand of them. He climbed up a high wooden tower, the conductor's stand, and from there surveyed his forces. His heart sank. He wished he were back in his quiet, lovely villa in Hietzing. He was convinced he would never survive that night.

Many accounts exist of the absurd adventure. The best was later written by Strauss himself:

In order to conduct the giant assembly of singers and orchestra members I had assigned one hundred sub-conductors. I could see only those who stood closest to me. In spite of our previous rehearsal it was impossible to think of giving an artistic performance. . . . Imagine my situation, in front of one hundred thousand wildly enthusiastic Americans. There I stood on the highest platform. How would this thing begin, how would it end?

Suddenly there is a cannon shot – a subtle hint for us twenty thousand to begin *The Blue Danube*. I give a sign. My hundred sub-conductors follow me as fast and well as they can. And now there begins a terrific racket which I won't forget as long as I live. Since we all had started at approximately the same time, I did all I could so we would all finish at approximately the same time. Somehow I managed to do it – it was really the only thing I could do. The audience cheered. The noise was fantastic.

I took a deep breath when I was outside again in the fresh air and felt firm ground under my feet. The following morning I tried to avoid a number of impressarios who promised me the whole of California for a tour of America. . . .

The Boston music critics agreed it was impossible 'to judge extraordinary events except by extraordinary standards and rules'. *The Herald* said that 'the chief honours from a strictly musical point of view were carried off by Herr Strauss whose activity, firmness and judgement make him a model conductor . . .'. It was also noted that he 'became a victim of the encore nuisance which attained proportions little short of monstrous'. They obviously had not been at his debut at Dommayer's when the critic Wiest deserted the crowded hall after the nineteenth repeat of the *Sinngedichte Waltz*.

The giant auditorium in Boston where Strauss conducted fourteen concerts to audiences of over one hundred thousand.

Somehow Strauss found time in Boston to write the *New Jubilee Waltz* which ended with a waltz arrangement of the *Star Spangled Banner*. The critics said he was 'magnetic', 'mercurial', 'dazzling', 'brilliant', 'electrifying' and 'irresistible'. In Vienna a newspaper informed its readers that Strauss was the first king to rule over America, and the Americans were said to have compared Strauss to Fulton, the inventor of the steamboat, calling the Strauss galop 'a steam dance'. 'In response to general request' he consented to conduct two balls. The orchestra was rather small by local standards, only three hundred men. He also conducted four concerts at the Opera House in New York, where people were jealous 'of the musical tornado in Boston' and the papers 'wrote rude things about it'.

On 13 July the Strauss party returned on the North German Lloyd ship *Donau*. At the head of the passengers' list it said, 'Mr Johann Strauss, with wife and servants, from Vienna'. Ten days later they were told in Bremen that there was an outbreak of the cholera in Vienna. The news was too much for Strauss, who could not stand the thought of sickness, and they went instead to Baden-Baden where Strauss had a standing invitation to conduct. After protracted stops in Mainz and Heidelberg they arrived in Baden-Baden where from time to time Strauss was seen walking in the casino gardens with an old admirer, Kaiser Wilhelm I of Germany. The Emperor wanted to hear his favourite Strauss waltzes – *Morning Papers, Artist's Life* and *Tales from the Vienna Woods* – time and again. He gave Strauss the Red Eagle Order, Strauss gave his fee to charities, and everybody was pleased, including the casino management: Strauss gambled and quickly lost some of the dollars he had earned in America.

13
The Operetta

One day in 1864 during the Vienna *Fasching*, Offenbach, who had dominated the musical scene since arriving in Vienna in 1858, told Strauss, 'You ought to write operettas.' It was a casual remark, and Strauss probably did not pay much attention to it – he was a waltz composer. 'A single waltz by Johann Strauss,' Wagner had written the preceding year in an essay about the reform of the Vienna Opera, 'surpasses in grace, elegance and genuine musical content most of the painfully imported foreign factory products' – referring to Offenbach, whom he hated. Offenbach was not only a Jew, but had committed the unpardonable crime of parodying Wagner.

It was certainly not Offenbach's casual remark but his success in Vienna which finally made Strauss write for the stage. It was also the right time. Since the middle of the century, immigrants had come to Vienna from the provinces of the Habsburg Empire – Bohemia, Moravia, Hungary, Serbia, Italy. Between 1860 and 1890, the populations of Paris and London increased by 60 and 62 per cent respectively, while Vienna's increased by 259 per cent. Vienna had 360,000 inhabitants in 1840 and two million in 1910 – more than today. The new immigrant population was attracted by the cosmopolitan features of operetta with settings in France, Italy, Hungary. The music might contain a Bohemian polka, a Polish mazurka, a Hungarian csárdás. And there was always the blissful Viennese mixture, the waltz.

Despite the opportunity Viennese operetta missed its big chance. It has been said that 'Viennese operetta substituted cosiness for gaiety, stupidity for nonsense, idle chatter for wit'. Paul Henry Lang enumerated 'the germs which were to ruin this type of the lyric stage: senseless action, insipid content, insincere feelings, laboriously invented jokes'. All are faults of the librettist, and Vienna never produced any such as France's Meilhac of Halévy. She had quite a few fine operetta

'In the Front Row at the Opera'
by William Holyoake.

composers. However, Strauss at his best was the best. Among the others there was Franz von Suppé (1819–95) from Dalmatia who had been inspired by Offenbach and brought a touch of Italy to Vienna. His finest works, *Boccaccio* and *Fatinitza*, are perhaps closer to comic opera. Karl Millöcker (1842–99) wrote lyrical masterpieces, *Der Bettelstudent (The Beggar Student)* and *Gasparone*. Carl Zeller (1842–98) belongs to the select company with *Der Vogelhändler (The Bird Catcher)*.

All of them died before the end of the nineteenth century and with them the brief, golden age of the Viennese operetta came to an end. Franz Lehár (1870–1948) created a short-lived renaissance with *The Merry Widow* in 1905 at the Theater an der Wien. He had the great gift of melody, a wonderful sense of rhythm, and his instrumentation is often brilliantly sophisticated. His late works, *Paganini* and *The Land of Smiles*, are almost operas, and it was probably significant that one of the finest operatic tenors of his time, Richard Tauber, who had started his career as a Mozart singer, was the star of many of his works.

After Lehár, however, Viennese operetta became almost a commercial product. There were some exceptions: Edmund Eysler, Leo Fall, Oscar Straus wrote some fine works, the best-known of which is *The Chocolate Soldier*, based on Shaw's *Arms and the Man*. Nevertheless, often operettas were artificially assembled by groups of librettists and arrangers, a theatre was leased and the operetta was produced and played night after night until it had lost its appeal. The Viennese operetta never made a successful comeback.

Seen in retrospect Strauss's initial reluctance to write for the stage was justified. His sound instinct told him to leave the theatre alone. Of his sixteen operettas, only two have remained durable successes – *Die Fledermaus (The Bat)* and *Der Zigeunerbaron (The Gipsy Baron)*. They and his great waltzes are performed time and again. Moreover, Strauss felt that he was fundamentally a waltz composer, not a musical dramatist.

Hanslick once wrote that in the operettas of Strauss 'the waltz stops the action'. Hanslick understood the laws of the stage. Strauss never learned them. He had no sense of drama, although occasionally he managed to turn a waltz theme to dramatic purpose. However, he was not aware that the composer must always be intimately involved in the story and its characters, and he had no real feeling for words. They meant little to him, except for the vowel sounds they contained because the vowels were the musical elements. He admired the great composers who understood the secrets of both drama and the music –

A fancy-dress evening at the Vienna Men's Choral Society with Liszt, Offenbach and Wagner among the guests.

Mozart, Verdi, Wagner – but he maintained that he did not belong in the theatre.

In the end it was Jetty Strauss, ambitious and resourceful, who succeeded by a ruse. She took some sheets of manuscript from the drawers in Strauss's desk – there were always piles of original pieces there that had not yet been performed – and brought them to Maximilian Steiner, the director of the Theater an der Wien since June 1869. He directed a few of his house-librettists to concoct a few scenes that would fit the music. When these were ready, Jetty brought her husband to the theatre to see and hear them. The material has since disappeared, but it fulfilled its purpose. Strauss was persuaded; it was always easy to persuade him. Steiner gave him a contract with a ten per cent royalty, but Strauss could have saved himself much heart-break had he turned the contract down and walked out of the theatre. He had spoiled his Viennese. They wanted his *Verzückungswalzer*, the delirious waltzes, his bewitching dance rhythms, and even during his operettas they were always waiting for the next great waltz, thus missing much of the fine music he wrote in between.

On 19 October 1869, Jetty wrote to a friend, '. . . Jean has offers from London and America where they would give him 300,000 francs for five months, but nothing will come of it. He wants to work this winter on an operetta for the Wiedner Theater.' The operetta was *The Merry Wives of Vienna*, written by Josef Braun, the librettist of Franz von Suppé. Not unlike an insecure Hollywood producer, Strauss would choose a librettist who had made a success elsewhere, not one who brought him what he thought was a good story. He composed the music quickly, working mostly at night. The operetta was never performed. Strauss wanted Josephine (Pepi) Gallmeyer, the diva and darling of the public, for the leading role, but she had left the Theater an der Wien after a row with Steiner, and went over to Karl Treumann at the Carl Theater. Strauss wanted no one else, and eventually with-drew the work, the score of which is now lost, although the book still exists.

The first act begins at midnight on New Year's Eve in Ring-strasse. Gas lamps, bells ringing, laughter, beautiful women, elegant men. It seems like a fine beginning, and Strauss probably wrote some beautiful music. He did not seem to mind at all that the project did not come off. He would have other ideas, maybe even better ones.

Steiner who had the contract with Strauss, assigned a whole team of librettists to collaborate with him. The method was very much like Hollywood in the golden 1930s when the contract with a star came first, and everything developed from there as illogically as possible. The libretto was first called *Ali Baba*, then *Fantasca*, later *Indigo*, and finally *Indigo or the Forty Robbers*. It was said in Vienna's coffee-houses that the forty robbers were the forty plagiarists who had contributed to the book. Strauss does not seem to have questioned the quality of the libretto, and he started on the music. This was shortly after the death of his mother and his brother Josef, and only work could help him to forget for a while. At the Theater an der Wien meanwhile the score was anxiously awaited.

On 10 February 1871 the premiere of *Indigo* took place at the Theater an der Wien. The programme said that the operetta was 'arranged for the stage, by Max Steiner from an old story'. No mention was made of the forty plagiarist-robbers. The performance had been scheduled for the preceding October, but was postponed because the Prussians defeated the French at Sedan on 1 September, and the consequences reverberated all the way to Vienna.

The first night of *Indigo*, now considered the beginning of the 'golden' era of the Vienna operetta, was a sensation. It was the first stage work by the uncrowned king of Vienna. The whole of Vienna was there. The critic Ludwig Speidel wrote about 'the scandalous prices' that touts asked for tickets. Even Johann Herbeck, the friend for whom Strauss had written *The Blue Danube*, and who had become director of the Court Opera, was unable to get a ticket and had to follow the performance from a chair among the musicians in the orchestra.

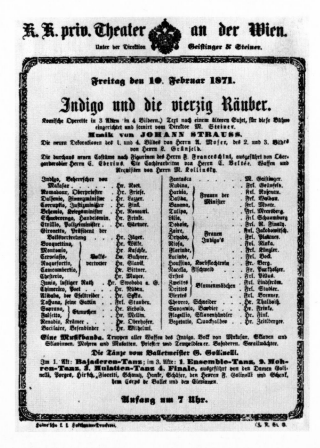

A programme of *Indigo* at the Theater an der Wien on 10 February, 1871.

ABOVE Jani Szika as Ali Baba in *Indigo*, and Marie Geistinger as Fantasca (RIGHT).

That night *Indigo* was a great personal success for its composer. Speidel writes that after the *pièce de résistance*, the waltz song ('Yes, that's how it is sung in the town where I was born'), the entire house 'uttered an ecstatic cry . . . people felt that Strauss should take the fiddle from one of the violinists, and play for the dancers, as he'd once done at Sperl's, at Zeisig's, at Dommayer's. Speidel correctly sensed that the people were nostalgic and also hungry for a new Strauss waltz. During the interval it was said that there was more excitement than at the Viennese premier of Wagner's *Die Meistersinger von Nürnberg*, earlier that month at the Court Opera. None the less a few critics took a more detached view. Hanslick admitted that the instrumentation was 'fine and piquant, ingenious in its harmonies and rhythms', and even quoted Goethe ('No work of art should be considered minor . . . when a great talent reaches the summit'), but he also noticed 'the sins of the libretto'. Four hours were much too long. The sets and costumes were beautiful, 'but Strauss should not write music for beautiful costumes'.

Hanslick was right. *Indigo* soon disappeared from Vienna. It was a success in Paris where they did not object to the libretto, and was later

186

performed in various versions. Eventually a new story was fitted to the music, and the operetta is still occasionally given under the title *A Thousand and One Nights*.

After *Indigo* Strauss was swamped with stories and librettos. Group libretto writing became a Viennese phenomenon. Would-be dramatists banded together to churn out texts. Some of them were strictly non-writers but ideas men who were unable to write a clear sentence. These were the precursors of the 'writing teams' of the Hollywood of the 1930s. In Vienna such teams often worked in a particular coffee-house where the atmosphere was said to stimulate the creation. Some people set up 'firms', and offered their products to the local composers, often at the same time playing one off against another. The short golden age of the Viennese operetta – the last three decades of the nineteenth century – came to an end for dramatic rather than musical reasons. There were gifted melodists there but few good librettists. Eventually the Viennese operetta became a contrived commercial product based on the lowest possible common denominator. Instead of dramatic action there was a senseless plot, instead of humour and wit there were tasteless jokes, instead of characters there were caricatures. Even gifted composers could not overcome such handicaps, especially if – as in the case of Strauss – they themselves had no dramatic instinct.

Why did Strauss accept so many bad librettos? Some critics thought he just did not understand the stage. Others implied that he did not sense the currents and cross-currents of his time. They were not important when he wrote for the ballroom, but essential when he began writing for the theatre. Once he asked a librettist for a certain character in a certain scene 'because I need a tenor in that scene'. Unfortunately the friends, advisers and consultants who surrounded him were no help. Jetty Strauss knew a little about the theatre from her own career, but placed no great faith in her own judgement. When the librettist Josef Braun (who had written the ill-fated *Merry Wives of Vienna*) suggested his new *Carnival in Rome* Strauss accepted at once. He liked the idea because the leading man was a painter, which proved his deplorable lack of dramatic instinct. Painting cannot be dramatized on the stage. Puccini, who really understood the stage, made the hero of *La Bohème* a romantic poet who sings poetic arias. Marcel, the painter, is used for dramatic contrast and atmosphere. Strauss also liked the Italian setting, the Roman carnival. A born melodist, he always loved Italy, the land of melody.

Carnival in Rome had its premiere at the Theater an der Wien on 1 March 1873. People liked the music, and they cheered Marie Geistinger, the leading lady. Ludwig Speidel, the critic, wrote what many listeners felt, 'The work is really divided into two parts – one

with the rhythms of a comic operetta, the other in the style of the lyric opera'. It was Strauss's first flirtation with his great unrequited passion: opera. His friend Johann Herbeck, who was then director of the Vienna Court Opera, had been tempted to produce *Carnival in Rome* as a comic opera at his house, but the theatre authorities and court councillors refused to consider having operetta in the hallowed opera house.

Two months later, on 1 May, the great Vienna Exhibition was opened. It was said to cover 'five times the area of the former Paris Exhibition'. Emperor Franz Joseph I, the Empress Elisabeth and the Crown Prince Rudolph were at the opening, and many crowned heads had also come. For the first and last time since the Congress of Vienna in 1815 the city was once more the glamorous 'capital of Europe'. The Court Opera performed Wagner and Gounod, and the Theatre an der Wien sold out whenever *Carnival in Rome* was given. Strauss wrote a choral waltz for the Exhibition, *Bei uns z'Haus (With us at home)*. Vienna was Europe's home, and Strauss its receptionist.

188

GRAND SUCCÈS DU THÉÂTRE DE LA RENAISSANCE
La REINE INDIGO
OPÉRA-BOUFFE
EN 3 ACTES
4 Tableaux
Paroles de
M.M. A. JAIME
ET
V. WILDER
Musique
DE JOHANN STRAUSS
DE VIENNE
PARIS, AU MENESTREL 2bis Rue Vivienne HEUGEL & Cie Editeurs

On 8 May, exactly one week after the opening, the 'Black Friday' crash of the Vienna Stock Exchange ended the era of the glorious though somewhat unhealthy Ringstrasse boom, and ruined many Viennese and foreign speculators, including those who had come to Vienna from Paris after the breakdown of the Second Empire. Shares became worthless, firms were wiped out; the shock waves of the panic were felt all over Europe and even in South America. There was a wave of suicides in Vienna, and a violent wave of anti-semitism among the small savers who lost their money. Karl Lueger, the brilliant politician and demagogue who became mayor of Vienna in 1897 (and was much admired by Hitler) for years kept telling the people that the crash had been the fault of the Jews. He failed to mention that many Jews had lost their money as well.

Things must really have been bad. The newspapers reported that for a while even the dance halls and *Heuriger* inns were deserted. And just at a time when so many foreigners had come to Vienna. One chronicler wrote that Vienna, 'invited the world to a wedding feast that turned into a funeral'. When a band passed the Stock Exchange playing *The Blue Danube*, some bystanders with a macabre sense of humour yelled, 'Go on, look at your damn blue Danube, it's full of dead bodies!'

Several weeks later Strauss wrote a beautiful new waltz, *Wiener Blut (Vienna Blood)*, which later became the title of a posthumous Strauss operetta. *Carnival in Rome* was now doing well, and the dance halls were crowded again, and people said, 'Vienna remains Vienna'. Late that year, after a succession of improbable events, Strauss began working on *Die Fledermaus*.

OPPOSITE A cover to the music of *Indigo*.
PREVIOUS PAGES 'Early Spring in Vienna Woods' by F. G. Waldmüller.

Sketches on the cover of *Wiener Blut*.

DIE FLEDERMAUS
WALTZES

ON MOTIVES FROM THE
CELEBRATED COMIC OPERA
BY

J. STRAUSS.

ENT. STA. HALL.

PRICE 4/=

LONDON.
ENOCH & SONS. 19. HOLLES S? CAVENDISH SQUARE W.

14
The Masterpiece

Great success sometimes arrives by a devious route. The strange story of *Die Fledermaus*, Johann Strauss's masterpiece, began with a farcical comedy, *Das Gefängnis (The Prison)* by Roderich Benedix, first performed in Vienna in 1851. The farce was read by Meilhac and Halévy in Paris, who based an amusing play on it, *Le Réveillon*, set on Christmas Eve, when the French traditionally celebrate by staying up and making merry. This comedy of confusion was a great success in 1872 at the Palais Royal in Paris. It was a year since the French had been defeated by the Germans, and people in Paris were trying to forget their worries. Meilhac and Halévy, astute satirists, had drawn a devastating caricature of the pre-war society – drinking, dancing, trying to out-do reality. It was the right play in the right place at the right time.

In Vienna Max Steiner heard of the success of *Le Réveillon* in Paris, and bought the rights for the Theater an der Wien although he had not even seen the play. When he read the script at last, he realized that it was 'too Parisian' for the taste of the Viennese. He unsuccessfully tried to sell it to his competitor, Franz Jauner of the Carl Theater. He seemed stuck with an unsaleable commodity. Then Gustav Lewy, the publisher and close friend of the composer, had a bright idea: why not try to turn it into a libretto for Strauss?

By another stroke of good luck the two to whom Steiner delegated the job were able men. Richard Genée from Danzig was not only a conductor at the Theater an der Wien, he was also a writer, and composed and arranged music. Moreover he understood the stage; he knew what a good operetta libretto should be. Karl Haffner from Königsberg had written several plays, but his contribution to the libretto was probably smaller than Genée's. Thus the words of the greatest Viennese operetta were written by two Prussians – people for whom the Viennese traditionally had little sympathy.

OPPOSITE A score cover to *Die Fledermaus*.

Jani Szika as Eisenstein in
Die Fledermaus.

Genée and Haffner soon realized that a simple rewrite of *Le Réveillon* was not suitable. They invented a new story around some of the farcical happenings, neutralized time and place (it was now anytime, anywhere), and created a new character, Dr Falke, the guiding spirit of the ensuing madness.

Contrary to most dramatic actions, the incident on which *Die Fledermaus* pivots occurs before the curtain goes up. Once Dr Falke and his friend, Gabriel von Eisenstein, known as a 'financier' (a glamorous profession during the days of the Ringstrasse boom in Vienna), went to a fancy dress ball – Eisenstein as a butterfly, Falke as a bat. After a wild night Falke woke up with a headache, lying under a tree in a wood outside the town. Eisenstein dropped him there at dawn, thinking it was great fun. Not for Falke, however, who had to walk home in broad daylight in his silly bat costume, attracting much attention and ridicule. Ever since Falke has been waiting to get even with Eisenstein. At the rise of the curtain he is ready.

Eisenstein tells the story only in the second act, and most people pay little attention to it. In fact a high proportion of most audiences are unaware of the connection between the operetta and its title.

Early in the first act Falke invites Eisenstein to a masked ball that night at the house of the rich Russian Prince Orlofsky, where Eisenstein, the typical elegant *belle époque* boulevardier, will meet many beautiful women. Eisenstein happens to be already married to a very beautiful woman, Rosalinde, but Falke says, 'She doesn't have to know.' Unfortunately Eisenstein is about to serve a short prison sentence for being disrespectful to an official, and the sentence starts that night. 'Never mind,' says Falke temptingly. 'You can report tomorrow.' While Eisenstein goes to change for the ball, Falke lets Rosalinde in on his plan and invites her to the ball where she can catch her husband red-handed.

The confusion is confounded by the unexpected appearance of Alfred, a former boy-friend of Rosalinde. The librettists had the good idea of making Alfred a tenor. Tenors always had their amusing side. They were often in love, mostly with themselves, vain and not exactly deep thinkers. After Eisenstein has kissed his wife good-bye and left for prison – in tails and white tie – Alfred comes back to the house. For one night he hopes to play the part of Rosalinde's husband, and he puts on Eisenstein's dressing gown. Just as he begins to enjoy the lost paradise, Frank the prison governor, comes to fetch Eisenstein. He finds what he thinks is a cosy domestic scene. Alfred is taken for Eisenstein, and goes to jail. Rosalinde gets dressed, and is off to the ball where she will meet her husband. She is disguised as a Hungarian countess, wearing a mask, and is displeased when she discovers that Adele, her maid, is also there, wearing one of her own best dresses.

Eisenstein has a weakness for Adele. There are pleasant cross-currents of eroticism – will she? won't she? – which put the bubbles into the *Fledermaus* champagne, but it is all sophisticated and a little bourgeois.

A fine comedy situation, then. Disguised lovers have long been stock characters in the Italian *commedia dell'arte*, in French plays and in Hungarian farces. Genée and Haffner had the brilliant idea of writing the whole story around the second act – the ball at Prince Orlofsky's. They knew that dance music was Strauss's great strength, and that Act II would give him the maximum opportunity to do what he was best at. The third act, in prison, is the most amusing blend of hangover and mistaken identity ever shown on the stage, for which the librettists invented the character of Frosch, the wonderfully witty, drunken jailer. Actually most characters are convincing as human beings, yet with a light farcical touch: Eisenstein, Rosalinde, the tenor Alfred, Adele, the blasé playboy Orlofsky. Towards the end, the comedy for a short moment approaches the borderline of near-tragedy when Eisenstein finds out about his wife and the tenor, but he is as graceful about it as Mozart's Almaviva in *Figaro*, who went out to deceive and ended by being deceived.

Carl Adolf Friese as Frank, the prison governor, and Alfred Schreiber as the drunken jailer, Frosch.

Die Fledermaus has been compared to *Le Nozze di Figaro*, but Genée and Haffner were not Beaumarchais. There is no hint of social criticism, no revolutionary undertone. At best it is a suave carnival joke that comes off brilliantly. In spirit it is French, and the music is Viennese, Johann Strauss at his best. No finer operetta combination was ever created. If I were to take just one operetta with me to that desert island, it would be *Die Fledermaus*.

Strauss seems to have felt a rapport when he started writing the music. He could identify with the characters, he knew the locale – he had seen the glitter and charm of Paris – and he understood the complications that could be expressed in waltz themes. The score is full of invention, charming, delightful from beginning to end, and the overture has been compared to the best of Auber and Adams.

Strauss was delighted with the libretto. He had some minor objections: he didn't like the title ('No one likes a bat'), and he was not certain that a prison scene between a drunken jailer and a prison governor with a hangover was in good taste. However, he overcame his objections, and literally flung himself into the work. He was in a frenzy of creation for forty-two nights, and Jetty wisely kept everyone away. Even his closest friends were asked not to disturb him. Steiner and Genée were the only visitors at the villa in Hietzing during these weeks. Strauss would play some of the new music for them. And he always listened to suggestions – too much maybe. At the beginning of the third act he had written some brilliant music for the orchestra, accompanying the pantomime of Frank, the prison warder returning from the ball, a wonderful study of the morning-after. During the rehearsal he heard Marie Geistinger's remark, 'If no one says something for such a long time, it gets boring.' Strauss immediately wanted to cut the scene. Fortunately Genée insisted that it must stay in; Genée realized the psychological subtlety of the music. Strauss's problem was that he created instinctively, and was never sure of himself. He would listen too much to the advice of others, and mostly it was bad advice. Some people warned him not to write a czárdás for the aria of the Hungarian countess (Rosalinde in disguise) at Orlofsky's. They said only a Hungarian could write a genuine czárdás. Since then many Hungarians have agreed that, while Strauss's may not be the genuine article, it is nevertheless a wonderful Austrian imitation.

Another ineradicable legend claims that the operetta was a failure when it was first performed at the Theater an der Wien, on 5 April 1874. The police had asked Steiner to delete one sentence from the part of Orlofsky, 'In my palais every lady may dress or undress as she likes,' and cut one verse from Adele's couplet in the last act, 'Of course I'm not faithful to my Marquis/ And have my Adolf besides.' The reviews were not good. Hanslick, making a major mistake, called the score 'a potpourri of waltz and polka motives'. H. Wittmann suggested that Strauss must not be praised too much 'or he might become impertinent. His talent is limited, and his music is a *musichetta....*' (At this point Rudolf von Procházka, Strauss's devoted biographer, reminds his readers that after the Berlin premiere of Mozart's *Don Giovanni*, in 1796, one critic summed it up, 'The work hurts reason, offends decency, and tramples upon virtue.') Only the *Morgenpost* critic noticed that 'one could get seasick in the orchestra stalls, as the people were swaying from side to side with the enchanting melodies'. That was a minority opinion.

Die Fledermaus was given sixty-eight times at the Theater an der Wien, not sixteen times, as many biographers report. It was not a success, but it was certainly not a failure. On 21 November 1874, seven months after the Vienna premiere, it was performed in New York, and two years later in London. It was given over a hundred times in Berlin, and conquered Paris after some complications. Meilhac and Halévy tried to keep 'their former *Réveillon*' from the stage, despite the fact that they themselves had initially taken their ideas from *The Prison* by Benedix. Two French librettists, A. Delacour and V. Wilder, completely rewrote the text, and Strauss foolishly let himself be persuaded to add some music from *Cagliostro*. The new version, called *The Gipsy*, was a great success. Today the work is popular in France under the original title, translated as *Le Chauve-Souris*.

There was some gossip in Vienna that much of the *Fledermaus* music had been written by Josef Strauss who had died four years earlier. It was said that Strauss had used material left by his brother. The gossip was revived in 1906, when Eduard Strauss published his *Memoirs*, with some vague, unsubstantiated hints. Serious musicians never believed a word of it. 'The orchestration proves the unique art of Johann Strauss,' says Professor Racek. 'The master's brush work is all over it.' 'Only a man who heard Offenbach's music earlier in Paris could have written this work,' writes Decsey. 'The erotic sophistication has a certain Gallic charm that was never part of the genius of Josef.'

Julius Korngold, Hanslick's successor as music critic of *Neue Freie Presse*, remembers an evening when he was very young, attending a performance of a new Offenbach operetta, *Die Tochter des Tambour-Majors (The Drum-Major's Daughter)*, at the Theater an der Wien. Strauss and his third wife, Adele, were sitting nearby. At a certain moment, when the melody sounded very much like the Fledermaus song, 'Oje, oje, wie rührt mich das,' Strauss smiled, and whispered to Adele, 'That's from my *Fledermaus*.' He was pleased;

The programme of *Die Fledermaus* at the Theater an der Wien.

gemalt von Herrn A. Brioschi

Anton Brioschi's set design for
Die Fledermaus.

Offenbach would not have borrowed – even unconsciously – something that was not good.

The most brilliant *Fledermaus* was staged by Max Reinhardt in Berlin in 1929. The great producer knew that Strauss's music was too good to be touched, but he improved the work by clearing up some ambiguity in the book. The curtain went up during the overture, and Tibor von Halmay, the dancer, was seen fluttering across the terrace in the costume of a bat. Reinhardt had explained right away why the operetta was called *Die Fledermaus*. And he gave the part of Prince Orlofsky, originally created as a trouser role for a mezzo-soprano, to the great comedian, Oscar Karlweis, elegant, sophisticated, blasé, tired and very real. He did not play Orlofsky; he *was* Orlofsky.

Strauss himself designated *Die Fledermaus* an operetta. Thus it should not be called a comic opera. The question arose when some opera houses in Austria and Germany, concerned about their artistic dignity, wanted to give *Die Fledermaus* as a surefire box-office attraction but were worried about their prestige. A stupid, unwritten

200

law in the late nineteenth-century opera houses said that only true operas were worthy to be performed, and managers wanted to side-step the issue by announcing *Die Fledermaus* as a comic opera.

Even the august Vienna Court Opera had to swallow its pride. It took twenty years for the director, Wilhelm Jahn, to accept the work in 1894. Fortunately Strauss was still alive, and the performance at the Court Opera was one of the great satisfactions of his life. In the beginning *Die Fledermaus* was given only in the afternoon, as a sort of popular matinee.

When Gustav Mahler became director in 1897, he ordered *Die Fledermaus* to be performed in the evening. He had produced and conducted the work in Hamburg, and loved it. Nowadays the work is regularly the New Year's Eve gala attraction at the Vienna State Opera, usually at top prices. Can there be a better way of winding up the old year and starting the new one?

On 5 May 1874, four weeks after the premiere of *Die Fledermaus*, La Scala announced a 'gran concerto di Giovanni Strauss di Vienna colla sua orchestra'. Strauss was with the Langenbach Orchestra from Germany and his friend Gustav Lewy on a tour of Italy where the public always wanted *The Blue Danube, Morning Papers*, and *Pizzicato Polka*. People loved Strauss and he loved Italy, and wrote a beautiful new waltz, *When the lemons blossom*, Opus 364, after Goethe's poem *Mignon*. Strauss had discovered the magic of Italy where problems are often diluted by sunshine, and he felt happily surrounded by melody. Theodor Billroth, the great Viennese surgeon and a friend of Brahms, was in Italy shortly after Strauss. He wrote to Hanslick that 'everybody here is singing the melodies of Strauss just as, not so long ago, everybody in Vienna sang Italian melodies.' The melodies of Strauss passed the supreme test in the country of melody and cantilena. The Italians, who had not much reason to like Habsburg Austria, completely accepted Strauss.

When he came back to Vienna, Genée and Camillo Walzel (the able librettist who wrote under the pseudonym F. Zell) discussed a new operetta idea, *Cagliostro in Vienna*, with him. The story was about the Italian adventurer, Cagliostro, who comes to Vienna during the centenary celebrating the victory over the Turks in 1684. Instead of the timeless comedy of *Die Fledermaus* he now had a rococo one set in Vienna with Italian characters. He would try something new: he would combine Viennese sensuality with Italian melody. Strauss was also excited to have Alexander Girardi, the greatest comedian in Vienna at this time, in the cast as the lovable rascal Blasoni. Girardi is still remembered there. He was the last great Austrian comedian after Raimund and Nestroy.

In spite of Girardi *Cagliostro in Vienna* was only a *succès d'estime*

Johann Strauss's sketches of Gustav Lewy and his son.

when it was first performed at the Theater an der Wien on 27 February 1875. One newspaper reported that some people had left a concert with excerpts from *Götterdämmerung* conducted by Wagner that night, and came to the Strauss premiere 'to relax in a Viennese atmosphere'. Unfortunately Strauss had not brought off the mixture of Vienna's mood and Italy's melody that had seemed to him an infallible recipe when he started working on the score. The finest piece was the *Cagliostro Waltz*, Strauss's reverence to Verdi, yet completely Viennese. In this waltz he indeed had made the mixture jell. Girardi sang it, and had to repeat it several times.

In March Strauss went to Paris to conduct the French version of *Indigo* at the Théâtre de la Renaissance. The Parisians loved it, and Hanslick reported from Paris, 'Our Strauss makes a furore. . . . In the light temperament of this music the Parisian recognizes himself. "Comme cela est Viennois!" they exclaim happily.' The first-act finale had been 'enriched' by *The Blue Danube* with a French text by Jules Barbier, who worked on the librettos of *Faust* and *The Tales of Hoffmann*:

> *Danube d'azur – (Quels sont ces chants?)*
> *Plus clair qu'un ciel pur – (Ces doux accents)*
> *O fleuve adoré! – (Rasant la mer)*
> *O fleuve sacré! – (Plânant dans l'air)*

Not great poetry but a lot better than Josef Weyl's original German text. The next year Strauss revisited Paris to conduct the French version of *Die Fledermaus*. Again the success was extraordinary. He returned to Vienna in a euphoric state, and at once made a bad mistake of accepting an Offenbach-style libretto by two Frenchmen, Wilder and Delacour.

Prince Methusalem was an involved comedy about the intrigues of two mythical Italian duchies with the very Offenbach names of Ricarac and Trocadéro. The authors called the delegates of the two duchies (possibly with a graceful if invisible bow to Shakespeare's Rosenkranz and Gildenstern), Mandelbaum and Feuerstein. A perfect vehicle for Offenbach, but not for Strauss who could not write satire and parody. He did not even bother to wait for the German translation of the French text and followed the original as he wrote the music. He conducted the premiere on 3 January 1877 at the Carl Theater.

Even though the director, Franz von Jauner, was a close friend and mounted a good production, the critics were not deceived. They agreed that the only good thing was the final waltz, which had to be repeated three times. After the third performance he went to Paris again to conduct several balls at the Opéra. This time he went alone,

LA CHAUVE-SOURIS

Opérette en 3 actes (DIE FLEDERMAUS)

d'après H·MEILHAC et L·HALÉVY

Livret de PAUL FERRIER   Musique de JOHANN STRAUSS

A poster for the French production of *Die Fledermaus*.

because Jetty was unwell. At least that was the official reason.

In Paris Strauss became involved in the sort of controversy that has delighted the Parisians since 1752, when the quarrel about the rival merits of French and Italian music gave rise to the *Guerre des Bouffons (War of the Comedians)*. This time it started between the supporters of Olivier Métra, 'the Parisian Strauss' of the Third Republic, and the followers of Strauss, who was said to have made some critical remarks about Métra in particular and French music in general. When he was announced to conduct a ball at the Opéra, everybody hoped for a glorious scandal. However, the diplomatic Strauss disappointed them. He delivered a flattering, charming statement about French music and Métra, made a donation to a local musical organization, and all was well. Having received the Knight's Cross of the Légion d'Honneur from President MacMahon he returned to Vienna and to personal tragedy.

15
Tragedy-and Lili

It was no secret among the intimate friends of Johann and Jetty Strauss that their marriage had been on the rocks for some time. When they married fifteen years previously, it had not bothered Strauss that his wife was eight years his senior. His mother had had doubts, per- haps because she knew her eldest son so well, but she had kept quiet. She knew there would be no point in telling him. Through all these years Jetty had been his 'secretary, diplomatist, finance minister, impres- ario' and a devoted wife. He depended on her in many ways, and he had never been able to cope with the daily routine of life. She had caused him to write for the stage, and she had been deeply involved in his greatest success, *Die Fledermaus*. Some people in Vienna thought the three chords at the beginning of the overture, ta-ta-*ta* in E, E sharp and F sharp, was a veiled allusion to ' Jet-ty *treffts*' (Jetty-Treffz- does-it).

Yet now that Strauss was fifty-two, Jetty was nearly sixty – and she looked her age. Watching Strauss she felt much older. He was still extremely attractive – much more, in fact, than when she had married him. He was the idol of Vienna, the women adored him, and he was not immune to feminine flattery. Jetty tried to be sensible, and although she had no desire to know everything, she could not help hearing a great deal. Once he had never travelled without her. Now he had been in Paris alone. He had not even insisted that she come with him when she said she was unwell. It was the old story, but it is always new and painful when it is experienced first-hand. He began to go out alone, even in Vienna, leaving Jetty at the villa in Hietzing. He had bought a large house and the adjoining site in Igelgasse, in the aristocratic Fourth District, the Wieden, and was building a Venetian- style mansion there. It was a quiet street, less ostentatious and more distinguished than a Ringstrasse address, and only a few minutes' walk

OPPOSITE Angelika Dittrich, Strauss's second wife.

to the Theater an der Wien and the Musikverein. In 1900 Igelgasse was renamed Johann-Strauss-Gasse.

His close friends knew that the villa in Hietzing had become the scene of bitter arguments. Strauss had always accepted the two daughters Jetty had by Moritz Todesco, although he was never close to them, but he was definitely shocked when a young man showed up one day at the villa in Hietzing and called Jetty 'Mother'. He was even more shocked when he found out other things about Jetty's former life.

It would have been easier – and also Strauss might have been more understanding – if he and Jetty had had children of their own. Or if Jetty had told him everything before they got married. Yes, he might have understood, but Jetty had been afraid. She was proud and courageous – it must have taken some courage in those days to live in Moritz Todesco's house as the unmarried mother of two girls – but, when she fell deeply in love with Strauss, she did not dare take yet another chance. She had been wrong, and now it was too late.

The son demanded money, much money. First from her, and then from her husband, the 'rich' Strauss. Strauss was a generous man about money, but he was vain, and by deception Jetty had hurt him in the way a man can be most easily hurt. In the end there was an unpleasant scene, and the word 'blackmail' was uttered. The young man was told to get out and stay out. It was very hard on Jetty. She loved her husband, but the boy *was* her son.

Afterwards she and Strauss hardly spoke. He would spend much time with his friends at Dommayer's, discussing a new libretto and supervising the house in Igelgasse. There was to be a dining room, billiard room and his study on the ground floor, and a salon and several bedrooms on the second floor. From his study he would see a lovely little park.

One night Strauss returned late and found the household in a state of panic. Jetty had had a stroke and was unconscious. In the afternoon she had received a letter from her son. It is not known what it said, but its effect on Jetty was devastating. She died during the early hours of 8 April 1878.

Strauss's biographers have tried to explain his panic during the following hours. He turned around, 'leaving the house without taking even his hat', and rushed to see his sisters at the Hirschenhaus and his brother Eduard. He said he could not stay another hour in Vienna, he had to get away, now. He asked Eduard, the tough one, to make all necessary arrangements. And off he went to the railroad station, and took the first train to Italy.

In his *Memoirs* Eduard wrote, with irony rather than understanding, about Strauss's bizarre fear of death. Strauss, the poet of live-and-let-live, whose waltzes are the apotheosis of life, could not stand the thought of death. Yet his reactions show a lack of inner discipline and human dignity. He had not been at the funeral of his beloved mother. And he was not at the funeral of the woman he had once loved and who had been the faithful comrade of the past fifteen years.

He found no peace of mind in Italy, and soon returned to Vienna. He could not bear to go back to Hietzing where Jetty would seem present all the time, and he moved into an apartment at the Hotel Viktoria, not far from his new house in Igelgasse. There he met Angelika Dittrich, from Breslau (not from Cologne, as she claimed), who had come to Vienna to study singing. Kapellmeister Proch introduced them. 'Lili' was then twenty-eight, slim, blonde, blue-eyed, very much the German 'Gretchen' type, but not exactly naïve and innocent. There was a certain reserve which Strauss found erotic because he sensed what lay behind it.

(According to another version of the story he had known Lili for some time. Adele who later became Strauss's third wife told her friends about a letter from her father who wrote, 'The affair seems to be of older date, perhaps started already while Jetty was alive.')

Strauss had reached the crossroads when men are apt to make very silly mistakes. To his friends the whole thing was quite transparent – the way Lili played up to him, pretending to adore him. Some of his friends tried to talk to him, but soon gave up. Strauss did not want advice. He married Lili in September – less than six months after Jetty's death. They moved into the new house in Igelgasse, that had been decorated according to Jetty's ideas. Strauss also bought an estate in Schönau, near Lobersdorf in Lower Austria, where he was going to play the country squire. And wherever they went, he was proud of the attraction created by his beautiful, young wife. He did not hear people saying, 'He's twenty-five years older than she is,' but right then Strauss was much in need of youth and beauty.

During their honeymoon Strauss began working on *Blinde Kuh* *(Blind Cow)* which was probably his worst failure. Rudolf Kneisel's comedy about some marriage complications in German middle-class circles was hopeless. Strauss had no one's advice. Jetty was gone, and Genée did not work on the libretto. Lili was no help; she did not understand the stage. The premiere on 18 December 1878 was a terrible flop. Only the waltz *Do you know me?* has survived. The critics made fun of the idiotic text, and the Viennese, who had adored Strauss, made fun of their erstwhile idol.

There were no secrets in the city. Soon everybody knew that the honeymoon was over: that Lili had no patience with her husband, that she did not like it when he spent the evening in his study working instead of taking her out. She had no feeling for music; she had taken

Angelika Dittrich in middle age.

OPPOSITE ABOVE Strauss playing billiards with his friends.
BELOW A musical evening in the Strauss household with Brahms, Makart, and Girardi among the guests.

OVERLEAF The Opernring, a section of the Ringstrasse, with the Opera House in the centre of the picture.

singing lessons as other girls take piano lessons, because it was the done thing. Around the Ringstrasse the gossip was that Lili had complained about her husband being 'old', and the I-told-you-so prophets were delighted. All the people who had been jealous of Strauss and his success, were busy spreading the gossip – and there were many of them. The ultimate humiliation came when it was whispered that Lili was having an affair with another man. To make matters worse he turned out to be Franz Steiner, the new director of the Theater an der Wien which depended so much on Strauss.

Strauss was, of course, the last to find out. Finally his sister Anna told him 'what everybody in Vienna except you' had known a long time. It was a great day for his enemies. Strauss, the master of the erotic waltz, who had 'seduced' millions of women with melodies, apparently could not practise what he composed.

The Lili episode lasted five interminable years. It began with a failure, *Blind Cow*, in Vienna, and ended with a failure, *A Night in Venice*, in 1883 in Berlin. In between Strauss had his ups and downs but no real success. When his friend Gustav Lewy told him that Suppé had turned down Heinrich Bohrmann's libretto, *The Queen's Lace Handkerchief*, Strauss accepted the text. He was convinced that Suppé had made a mistake. The story was built around an improbable anecdote involving Cervantes and the handkerchief of the Queen of Portugal, who had written on it, 'A queen loves you, though you are no king.' The time was 1580. Strauss had always a strange liking for historical themes, and he wrote some beautiful music around this one. The waltz *Rosen aus dem Süden (Roses from the South)*, Opus 388, contains the Truffle Couplet from *Spitzentuch*, which helped to make the operetta a success – at least for a while.

The text for Strauss's next operetta, his eighth, was written by Genée and Zell. *Der lustige Krieg (The Merry War)* is a silly story, but people liked the music. Briefly, Violetta, the prima donna, is to marry the Duke of Nimburg who fights the Genoese. General Umberto from Genoa impersonates the Duke. Sent to marry Violetta by proxy, he marries her himself. Somewhere a Dutch bulb merchant named Groot appears impersonating the Duke. Curtain. That such nonsense was tolerated by a patient audience was due to Girardi. Having a rather small part, he had asked Strauss for a special number. For some reason Strauss refused, and there was a row. Strauss even threatened to give the part to another comedian, Karl Swoboda. Luckily for Strauss Swoboda was otherwise occupied, and Strauss had to play a few waltz motives for Girardi. He was not pleased when Girardi selected the *Naturwalzer* which became the great hit of the operetta when it was first given on 25 November 1881. It was repeated several times and saved the evening. The critic of *Neues Wiener Tagblatt* wrote,

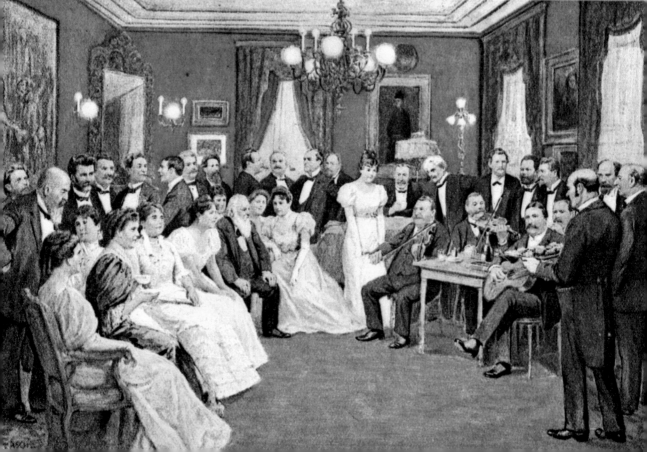

'It remains an unfathomable mystery why a musician of the greatness of Johann Strauss is so insecure about his very special field. . . .'

Two weeks after the premiere the worst disaster in Vienna's long theatrical history occurred. On 8 December 1881 a few minutes before the curtain was to go up at the second Viennese performance of *The Tales of Hoffmann* at the Ringtheater in Schottenring, fire broke out on stage. The night before (which Johann Strauss happened to attend) had been a great success. The house was sold out.

There was a terrible panic. The doors out of the auditorium opened inwards. A mass of people inside desperately pushed against them, trapped. At least 384 people were burned, asphyxiated or trampled to death. While the dead bodies were carried out, Anton Landsteiner, the police officer in charge of the rescue operations, reported to Archduke Albrecht, 'All saved, Your Imperial Highness', which remains the epitome of Viennese optimism for all time. Just then a subordinate whispered in Landsteiner's ear that more bodies had been found and were stacked up behind the ruins of the theatre. He waved him away. 'All saved' is still a by-word for the Austrian predilection for self-delusion.

Vienna was mourning the dead, but at the Theater an der Wien the performances of *The Merry War* went on. Girardi and Strauss amused their public night after night.

In 1882 Genée and Zell finished two operetta libretti, *The Beggar Student* and *A Night in Venice*. They offered both books to Strauss and also to the composer Karl Millöcker (1842–99). Both men wanted *The Beggar Student*. This did not surprise Genée and Zell, because they knew that *A Night in Venice* was rather a poor libretto. For this reason they decided that Strauss must do it. He might bring it off. In the hands of Millöcker, who was still rather inexperienced, it would be a disaster. Knowing that Strauss always wanted what somebody else had – no wonder, since he never trusted his own judgement – they claimed that Millöcker was crazy about *A Night in Venice*. That did it: Strauss took the bait. Millöcker later had a well deserved success all over the world with *The Beggar Student*, which remains one of the few great Viennese operettas. *A Night in Venice* is mercifully forgotten.

Strauss had been attracted by the idea of Goldoni's Venice – gondolas, intrigue, beautiful women, the Doge's Palace, music, and more music. It was the tragedy of Strauss as an operetta composer that he confused atmosphere with drama and mood with action. After the failure, he wrote to his friend Paul Lindau:

The book was so bad that with the best will I couldn't get inspired by it. It had neither poetic nor comical colour. There simply seemed to be no need for music . . . I never saw the libretto with the dialogues. All I had were the lyrics when I began working. During the final rehearsals, when I saw the

OPPOSITE The fire at the Ringtheater in 1881.

Rosa Streitman as Ciboletta in
A Night in Venice.

whole thing for the first time, I was appalled. No real feeling, no truth, no sense, nothing but nonsense from beginning to end. I know that the music doesn't fit the silly, artificial text . . . I hope the damn thing will soon wind up at an Old Folks' Home [*Versorgungsheim*]. I couldn't care less. . . .

It is hard to understand Strauss's frivolity. He knew how much trouble Verdi and Wagner took over their texts. He knew Mozart's famous letter to his father, dated 13 October 1781:

Why do Italian operas please everywhere in spite of their miserable libretti, even in Paris, where I myself witnessed their success? Just because the music reigns supreme, and when one listens to it all else is forgotten.

But the young Mozart also concluded that 'the best thing of all is when a good composer, who understands the stage and is talented enough to make sound suggestions, meets an able poet, that true phœnix'. Perhaps Strauss thought he could get away with it when his music reigned supreme. Yet once he wrote to Max Kalbeck that 'librettist and composer should sleep in one bed'. His career could be called a tragedy of bad libretti. Richard Specht writes, 'To compose a musical comedy without knowing the sequence of scenes, the mood out of which the arias develop – can one show more indolence for the dramatic?'

The famous tenor Girardi as Caramello in *A Night in Venice*.

The finale to the first act of
A Night in Venice from a
performance in 1883.

A Night in Venice was first given at the Friedrich Wilhelm
Städtisches Theater in Berlin on 2 October 1883. The Viennese
papers covered the occasion like war correspondents on a foreign
battlefield. Strauss and his friends were again worried about the
libretto. After a stormy all-night meeting he was advised not to
conduct, because there might be some barracking. Unfortunately he
decided he would conduct after all. The quick-witted Berlin audience,
less sentimental about Strauss than the Viennese, frequently burst
out laughing at the ludicrous plot. In the second act, when somebody
sang 'At night the cats are grey and sing tenderly miaou', people
laughed and booed. It was a first-rate theatre scandal. Strauss sat
through the noise, 'pale and trembling'. Even the finest part of the
score, the *Lagunenwalzer*, was no success there.

It was, however, a few days later at the Theater an der Wien, in
Vienna. The people cheered 'their' Strauss who had been so badly
treated in Berlin. And there was Alexander Girardi as Caramello. The
libretto was thoroughly panned, but 'the composer received praise',
wrote the *Theaterzeitung*.

Strauss was happy that night. He still had not quite lost his magical
touch. The *Lagunenwalzer* was one of his great successes. To his relief
Lili had left him the year before, but he was no longer alone: that
night Adele sat next to him.

216

16
Number 3: Happiness with Adele

He had known Adele Deutsch since she was a little girl with pig-tails. Her first husband's father, Albert Strauss – no relation – was a Jewish banker, a cultured 'Old Viennese', who had been a friend of Grillparzer and Nestroy. He always liked the company of writers, musicians, artists. He lived at the Hirschenhaus, and had become the friend and occasional financial adviser of the first Johann Strauss. Albert's son, Anton, had married Adele Deutsch, a charming Jewish girl from Vienna. Three years later he died, leaving Adele with a small daughter Alice.

Strauss met her in the street one day in 1881. He was still married to Lili but separated from her. He was fifty-six and still very attractive. The recent years of suffering had given him a new perspective of life: he no longer considered himself the darling of the gods. He was morbidly afraid of getting old. The sight of grey hair at the temples irritated him, and he dyed his hair black. No one ever saw him sloppily dressed; he remained fastidious about his appearance. His friends knew that 'he never wore a tie more than four times'.

He spent most of his time alone in his big house in Igelgasse, and he hated his loneliness. He began to see a good deal of Adele. He would visit his sisters at the Hirschenhaus, and drop in on Albert Strauss in the same house. By coincidence, no doubt, Adele would also be there. Soon he wanted to marry her, but there were problems. He would have to divorce Lili. Franz Steiner had not offered to marry her, as she had hoped, and she would make sudden, dramatic appearances at Strauss's house or in Schönau, and there were very unpleasant scenes. She regretted everything and 'wanted to come back'. It was difficult. Strauss had to ask his lawyers to settle things once and for all, but it was not easy. Even after a divorce he could not hope to marry Adele in Vienna: she was Jewish, he was Catholic, and Austrian law was very strict. After years of trying Strauss was told he would have to

'An evening with Johann Strauss' after an oil painting by Franz von Bayros. Brahms sits second from the left and Adele is to the left of Strauss at the piano. Eduard Strauss is on the far right of the picture.

give up both his religion and his citizenship, but he made sure that he would not lose his cherished title of *Hofballmusikdirektor* by embarking on so radical a course.

He had an influential friend, the Archduke Johann, who a few years later gave up his title and became Johann Orth. The Archduke discussed the problem with Duke Ernst II of Saxe-Coburg-Gotha who happened to be an admirer of Strauss, and as a result Strauss went to Coburg and became a member of the Evangelical Church. His friend, Dr Josef Trutter, a lawyer, helped with the complicated formalities. In a letter to Adele, Strauss wrote:

> The things one does for a woman. . . . Immediately after my arrival I had to see the *Oberbürgermeister*, the *Oberjustizrat*, the *Obermagistratsbeamte* . . . I took my legal residence here and became a citizen of Coburg . . . I had to sign some forms and say a few nice words to everybody . . . I send you millions of kisses, and hope to embrace tomorrow morning.

It was late in January 1887 that Johann Strauss became a citizen of Coburg. On 15 August he and Adele were married there. He gave to her an annuity for life of 4,000 guilders. (His tax return of 1888 exists. His income was 9,250 guilders; he had to pay 1,180 guilders in taxes, over one-eighth.)

We know much more about Adele Strauss than about his first two wives. She survived her husband by thirty-one years, and died in Vienna on 9 March 1930. After Strauss's death in 1899 his widow's only mission in life was to perpetuate his memory. She turned the house in Igelgasse into a Johann Strauss Museum, and published a selection of his letters, presided over memorials and generally tried to keep his name alive. The Viennese were perhaps not wrong when they called Adele, half-jokingly, 'Cosima in three-four time' – a reference to Richard Wagner's formidable widow.

Strauss admitted to his close friends that Adele gave him his 'third youth'. Adele said after his death, 'I never had the feeling of having married an old man.' His letters – at least those Adele permitted to be published – convey the impression that he was very much in love with her. Once he wrote to her, 'I stand before you immaculate from the moment I could call you mine. Can you think of another such artist on earth?' He certainly could not have made a similar assertion to Jetty. As though embarrassed by this display of intimate feeling he ends on a lighter note, 'Woman, be fair, and say, "There's only one *Kaiserstadt*, there's only one Jeany".' Another time he protested, 'I have remained faithful to you. I can swear it. Sometimes I myself am surprised about it, but it is no wonder: Adele has taken complete possession of my heart. I kiss you a million times.'

Sixtyish and mature, Strauss was deeply in love with her: 'You made me mad with happiness. I would like to jump. I even want to dance, though this would be difficult because I was never a dancer . . . let us be happy, Adele.' On another occasion he sent her a message from the theatre where he conducted,

I shall make an Allegro out of a Maestoso so I can be with you earlier. . . . Let us be happy, Adele, *on ne vit qu'une fois*. I embrace you innumerably. Your delirious

Jean

As a postscript he adds a few notes, the beginning of the *Cagliostro* duet, 'I wish I could fly with you through life . . .'.

A portrait of Adele, done by their friend Franz von Lenbach, shows an attractive, dark-haired woman, slim and erect, very sure of herself, certainly not the motherly housewife type. In many ways Adele picked up where Jetty had left off. (In Strauss's late years any mention of Lili was taboo.) Adele became Strauss's manager, and ran both him and his house efficiently, even attending to his correspondence. Strauss wrote good letters, but he did not always answer all those that he received. Letter writing was more of an effort than composing. Adele also looked after his press relations by judiciously courting certain important critics and pointedly ignoring others who

Adele Deutsch, the third wife of
Johann Strauss.

had been 'too critical'. She also decided who was going to see him, and
there was no appeal against her decision. She dropped some of his old
friends who seemed insufficiently important, and invited people who
might be useful. She knew that he was suffering more and more from
neuralgia as he got older, and that this accounted for his spells of
depression. He had inherited a touch of the Strauss family melancholy,
after his grandfather, father and brother Josef. She built a *cordon
sanitaire* around him and protected him – perhaps too much so in the
opinion of some people. In her drawing room Adele had a collection
of photographs with personal dedications: Bertha von Suttner, Jules
Massenet, Maurus Jókai, Anton Rubinstein and of two personal
admirers, Brahms and Alfred Grünfeld. In the dining room she
showed a predilection for busts: Brahms, Schubert, Girardi, Crown
Prince Rudolf, and there was a painting showing Strauss conducting
his father's orchestra for the first time at the Volksgarten in 1849.

Strauss rarely discussed musical problems with his friends. He
would play billiards or tarock with them, or walk in the woods, in
Ischl. Hadramovsky and Otte write:

Adele made him a sort of king – something Strauss, a natural, nervous
person, didn't want to be. . . . She led him on the way from the operetta to
the opera where he didn't belong. Trying to force his success, Strauss lost
himself in detail. While he was always looking for something new, trying to
reach for the stars, he lost the ground under his feet. . . . We cannot absolve
Adele from guiding him along this road, no matter how devotedly she
guarded his heritage for three decades after his death.

Unfortunately the latter years were one succession of jubilees and
celebrations, for the Viennese loved to honour their popular idol, at
the same time honouring themselves. The festivities were a severe
nervous strain for Strauss, and made him feel old – something he hated
more than anything else.

The fortieth anniversary of his debut at Dommayer's Casino was an
ordeal from beginning to end. In the morning on 15 October 1884 the
mayor paid an official call to present Strauss with the diploma that
made him an Honorary Citizen of Vienna, 'free of taxes'. Then
Girardi arrived, heading a delegation from the Theater an der Wien.
The Men's Choral Society came, the Academic Gesang-Verein, the
Society of Friends of Music, the Journalists' Association Concordia,
the Workers of Vienna, Eduard Strauss with the members of his
orchestra. Letters and telegrams from Brahms, Bülow, Verdi, Anton
Rubinstein, the Archduke Wilhelm, former President MacMahon,
Bismarck and others.

That night there was a special gala performance at the Theater an
der Wien with a monster programme 'personally conducted by the

composer': the *Indigo* Overture, the first act of *A Night in Venice*, the second act from *Die Fledermaus*, and excerpts from all the other Strauss operettas. The ovation terrified Strauss, who was forced to conduct *The Blue Danube* after the overture. An 'intimate' ceremony was to have taken place on stage after the audience had left, but since people remained in their seats cheering, and the curtain stayed up this 'private' party was exposed to the gaze of all Vienna. Camillo Walzel, the director, gave Strauss a jubilee medal. Strauss, asked to speak, managed to say just a few words: 'I am too deeply moved to express here what I feel . . . I thank you all, my beloved Viennese, from the depth of my heart.'

Still later there was a banquet at the Goldenes Lamm with two hundred prominent people attending. The menu featured *Schill* (pike-perch) *from the Blue Danube, Filets à la Cagliostro, Morgenblätter Salad* and *Ice Cream Indigo*.

In 1885, a year later, Strauss had his greatest operetta success since *Die Fledermaus* (1874). It had all begun in February 1883, when Strauss had been invited by the People's Theatre in Budapest to conduct the Hungarian premiere of *The Merry War*. He asked Adele Deutsch, not yet his wife, to accompany him. At dinner in the house of friends they met Liszt, who played piano duets with the hostess while Strauss

The Goldenes Lamm, where a banquet was held to celebrate the fortieth anniversary of Strauss's debut.

turned the pages. Then Strauss played his still unpublished waltz *Frühlingsstimmen (Voices of Spring)*, Opus 410, which he had originally written for Bianca Bianchi, a coloratura soprano, to a text by Richard Genée. When Bianchi sang it at the Theater an der Wien, critics said it was 'mediocre', 'not very melodious', and 'top-heavy with coloratura'. Like *The Blue Danube*, *Frühlingsstimmen* first made its mark abroad. It was a great success in Russia, where Strauss conducted it in 1886. In Italy it became a popular encore for other coloratura sopranos. Strauss made a piano arrangement which he dedicated to his friend Alfred Grünfeld, who played it with inimitable grace and made it world famous. The Viennese critics belatedly admitted that it was 'closer to Mozart and Schubert than to Lanner or Father Strauss'. Some said it would never be popular in the ballroom because it was not written for the violin. Strauss loved listening to Grünfeld: 'When you play my waltz it sounds more beautiful than when I wrote it,' he once said. Few composers make such admissions.

Later that night in Budapest, while the two composers were playing whist, Liszt was still ecstatic about the waltz which Strauss had played. A few days later Strauss and Adele met the Hungarian poet and novelist Maurus Jókai who told them of his novel *Saffi*, an eighteenth-century story about a beautiful gypsy girl. It sounded as if it could be the basis of just what Strauss needed more than anything else – a good libretto. Jókai was unwilling to write the libretto himself, but suggested his friend Ignatz Schnitzer, a Hungarian journalist living in Vienna.

Schnitzer turned out to be the answer to Strauss's prayers: he was a man of taste and imagination, who had dramatic talent and knew much about music. He had watched Strauss and his struggles with inept texts. He also knew that Strauss did not understand the stage, and did not really collaborate with his librettists. He therefore suggested a plan. Schnitzer would make a scenario from Jókai's novel, and then he and Strauss would discuss every character, every motivation, every scene, every song. Schnitzer wanted Strauss to be completely familiar with the mood at every moment of the play 'so that the music would fit the dramatic structure exactly'. Strauss would compose the music first, even the songs. Only then would Schnitzer write words to fit them.

Strauss wanted to stay young, but never played the fool with Adele as he had done with Lili. He shaved off his side whiskers but kept his moustache, turned up at the ends which was the fashion. In 1894, when he was sixty-nine, Eisenberg wrote of 'the Master's erect bearing, the healthy colour of his face, the dark rich hair, not a trace of baldness, looking thirty years younger'. He gives this impression in the portrait by Franz von Lenbach: there is a youthful look in his eye

OPPOSITE Johann and Adele Strauss.

and a slightly amused expression on his face. The man looks sure of himself, but we know this was not true. Alone in his study at night he only felt secure because Adele was in her bedroom two doors away. Even though he liked privacy, he hated isolation. In later years he said that they had never been separated for more than twenty-four hours during the sixteen years of their marriage.

Occasionally there was an argument, as this extract of a letter shows:

I wish you a very good night, Adele, good sleep and good humour on waking up. A sense of humour is worth more than the best medicine. My motto always was 'To walk through life merrily'. Nagging spoils health and life, and it spoils a woman's beauty (if she ever had any). Women should always try to smile. That makes them beautiful and keeps the wrinkles away. Enjoy life; cry only when there is really something to cry about. Your best friend

Jeany

Obviously Strauss had patience, wisdom and a sense of humour. He was able to smile at himself even in bad moments. In 1888 he went with Adele to Franzensbad, a Bohemian spa which was supposed to be good for barren women. Adele had her daughter Alice from her first marriage, but she hoped to have a child by Strauss. He did not like spa life, but he had to accompany Adele. He wrote to J.S. Priester, who took care of his financial affairs:

Adele had already 18 baths.
Jeany had 22 baths.
Boredom in Franzensbad. Terrible.
It's as cold as in Siberia, 7 degrees Centigrade.
Adele has a head cold.
The food here is horrible.
There are five and a half persons left in Franzensbad.
Our doctor is an idiot.
We try to avoid the spa orchestra.
Nothing but lies in the newspapers.
We still live together happily and *gemütlich*.
I need the librettists like a piece of bread.
Adele today wrote *no* letter to her mother.
Only Gentiles are still here.
Depressed about bad relations between Russia and Germany.
Austria will soon be beaten.

Another letter to Priester was scribbled in his study in Vienna on the back of a used envelope in the early hours of the morning, Adele having taken her daughter Alice to a ball. It consists of a number of chronological remarks:

Already 2 a.m. The woman [*das Weib*] not yet back.
The ball mother certainly seems to have fun!

2:15. Still not yet at home. I'm getting really frantic. [*Es steigen mir die Grausbirnen auf.*] These lines are written while I'm getting drunk.
2:30. Still without wife.
2:45. ditto.
3:00. ditto.
3:30. Just arrived! [Three times underscored.] Adieu.

Adele kept routine problems away from him. She knew he needed quiet and peace of mind. Strauss rarely went to bed before 2 a.m., and always got up around nine. In the morning he would sketch ideas, standing at a high desk. Sometimes he would break off to walk around, or play a solitary game of billiards. Adele gave strict orders to people in the house that he must not be disturbed during these hours. At night he would often orchestrate the ideas he had sketched in the morning. He might write a short letter to Adele which he placed on her bedside table for her to find when she woke up.

He loved to work when it was raining, because the sound was soothing to him. In 1894 he reports contentedly from his villa in Ischl to Priester:

Rain, nothing but rain and busy gurgling sounds of the nearby brook . . . infinitely wonderful. To write music in a well heated room, there is nothing more beautiful. I am happy to hear the crackling of the tiled stove. The worse it gets outside, the better I feel here. I want no sunshine while I work, but I admit that sunshine is sometimes necessary in life. . . .

It was an unorthodox but successful method. It worked so well that Strauss once asked Schnitzer 'to put as many a's and i's as possible into the *Dompfaff* duet, because the singers like these vowels'. Schnitzer forced Strauss to do what a composer must do if he wants to write successfully for the stage: to follow the dramatic structure exactly; to do what, on a higher level, Wagner and Verdi had done so convincingly. The result was an even higher degree of integration between words and music than in *Die Fledermaus*.

Schnitzer refused to let Strauss dash off the music in a few weeks. They worked for almost two years on *Der Zigeunerbaron (The Gipsy Baron)*. Like all good stories the plot is basically simple. The love story begins among the gipsies of Hungary and ends in Maria Theresa's Vienna, a not illogical progress when one remembers that the Emperors of Austria were also Kings of Hungary. In 1867 the Emperor Franz Joseph and his Empress had actually been crowned in Budapest. (Hungarians still think of Franz Joseph as 'The King'.) It was an audacious experiment. Franz Joseph had vainly hoped that the Dual Monarchy might safeguard the future of the Habsburg Empire, but, while it temporarily appeased the Hungarians, the experiment irritated the other members of the Imperial family and of nations, particularly the Czechs, and eventually it led to the fall of the monarchy.

When, however, Schnitzer and Strauss worked on *The Gipsy Baron* in 1885, there was still hope the experiment might succeed. Both the Hungarian Schnitzer and the Austrian Strauss believed in it, and they succeeded in creating the synthesis of Schnitzer's beloved Hungarian folklore and Strauss's beloved Vienna, for the operetta became musically the epitome of Austria–Hungary, the Dual Monarchy. They worked hard on it. Their correspondence gives us the only insight into Strauss's dramatic thinking, limited as it was. Here are some samples:

Much depends this time on the first couplet of Girardi. He must immediately win sympathy, charm the people. . . .

Did you confer about the third act with Jauner? I hope he will spend enough on the sets. . . .

The march couplet must be so short that it can be repeated three times if the people like it. Remember Suppé's march-terzetto in *Fatinitza* which was almost always repeated three or four times, and wouldn't have had that success if it had been longer than it is.

I like all the lyrics except the hog-breeder's couplet. . . . But you're going to have an idea, I'm not worried. You are a jack-of-all-trades, a wonderful creator. . . .

From Berlin, where he had conducted, he wrote to Schnitzer:

The entrance march must be magnificent. At least a hundred soldiers, people in Hungarian, Viennese, even Spanish costumes, women, children with flowers – it must be a wonderful scene, since we this time show our soldiers and the people after a victory, happy and exuberant. . . . I have a feeling, dear friend, that Gipsy Baron will make us richer than 100,000 Rothschilds.

Strauss knew instinctively that this time he was working on something of enormous potential, and spared no effort. His personal life was happy at this time. He was married to his dear Adele, and Lili and the consequences, in Coburg and elsewhere, were forgotten. Indeed, he worked with such frenzy that the doctors forbade him to do any composing while he was with Adele in Franzensbad. But after his return to Vienna he told Schnitzer, 'I would memorize a few of your lyrics before going on a solitary long walk in the woods, and there I would write the melodies on my starched cuffs.' And he wrote the last act in three days in Ostend where he had allegedly gone to relax. Meanwhile Schnitzer was forever trying to improve the lyrics,

Theo Zasche's drawing of the
first performance of
The Gipsy Baron.

LEFT AND BELOW Costume
designs for *The Gipsy Baron* by
Karl von Shir.

changing details, until he wrote to Strauss, 'Happy is the librettist when there is nothing to be changed anymore.'

Strauss was secretly hoping to have the work performed at the Vienna Court Opera. There was only one ambition left in his life: to write an opera. He consciously created certain sections – the first-act finale, the trio in the second act and some of the arias – in operatic style. *Wer uns getraut?* was long considered an operatic aria. *The Gipsy Baron* was given to the Theater an der Wien, however. Jauner, who prepared the production with great care, went to Hungary and there bought authentic costumes and other articles from the gipsies. 'Our gipsy village must be so realistic that the people in the auditorium will involuntarily put their hands in their pockets to be sure they cannot be picked.'

The dress rehearsal did not go well, and Strauss's friends feared another failure. At a party in Jauner's house on the eve of the premiere most people kept conspicuously away from Strauss and his wife. They were wrong. The first performance, on 24 October 1885 – one day before his sixtieth birthday – was Strauss's greatest success since *Die Fledermaus*. He conducted, and was received with ovations which continued throughout the performance. Almost all numbers had to be repeated. Girardi, the hog-breeder Zsupan, was – after Strauss – the star of the evening. He was magnificent, returning as a soldier from Spain, wearing a long red coat. When he opened the coat, the delighted audience saw that his belt was hung with knives and watches. No one would have dared predict then that exactly sixty years later soldiers wearing a different uniform would carry a dozen wrist watches on their arms that they had taken away from the Viennese.

Girardi's Zsupan remained one of his greatest roles. It did, with the help of Schnitzer and Strauss, more for the rapprochement between Austrians and Hungarians than most diplomats, political writers and politicians were able to do. Strauss later wrote to Girardi, 'On your shoulders every work rests, and the very existence of the Theater an der Wien. . . . You alone decide about to be or not to be.' A dangerous admission to make to an actor, but it was justified, and Girardi took no advantage of it. In Bad Ischl, where both men spent their summers, Strauss would often send a footman across the street to Girardi in the middle of the night. Both were reserved, almost shy. Only after working together for years did they address one another with the familiar *du*.

The critics, as always, could not agree. While the *Fremdenblatt* said it was impossible to report 'how many times the Meister had to come before the curtain after each act', Hanslick remarked that 'in the second-act finale Strauss has strayed close to the dangerous borderline

Girardi in one of his greatest
roles as Zsupan in
The Gipsy Baron.

of grand opera'. Max Kalbeck hoped that 'now we would perhaps
soon greet Strauss at the opera house'. *The Gipsy Baron* was eventually
performed at the Vienna Opera, but only after Strauss's death.

Schnitzer also predicted, 'Unless I am mistaken, we'll make a lot
of money with *The Gipsy Baron*.' Neither he nor Strauss was mistaken.
After eighty-nine performances during the initial run it became the
prototype of the many imitations in the Austro-Hungarian style that
were churned out in Vienna. With very few exceptions – such as
Franz Lehár's *Zigeunerliebe (Gipsy Love)* and Emerich Kálmán's *Die
Czardasfürstin (The Csárdás Princess)* – none came even remotely close
to the work of Schnitzer and Strauss. It was performed all over the
world.

Strauss had, nevertheless, learned nothing from his collaboration with Schnitzer on *The Gipsy Baron*. Schnitzer had suggested a play, *Der Schelm von Bergen*. Strauss was so attracted by the leading character, a sympathetic executioner who dislikes executions, that he sat down and began working on the score, but then he found out that a similar character had appeared the year before in *The Mikado*, and he gave up the project. He still saw Schnitzer frequently, but unfortunately he did not listen to Schnitzer's advice. His professional advisers always talked of a libretto that 'would please the public'. 'Instead of thinking of a good story they were concerned with what they thought the audience wanted,' writes Max Kalbeck. When Strauss heard about the success of a German romantic opera, *Der Trompeter von Säckingen*, by Victor Nessler, he told his scouts to look for a similar subject – a folk play that would need simple, popular melodies. He behaved exactly as the men in Hollywood during the 1930s and 1940s who believed in cycles of success.

A poster of the
three-hundredth
performance of
The Gipsy Baron at the
Theater an der Wien.

Gustav Lewy told him about a young librettist, Victor Léon, who had been very successful with *Der Doppelgänger (The Double)* in Munich. Léon had good ideas about revolutionizing the stage and 'trying to write serious operetta'. This was the advent of naturalism in Germany. The young playwright was invited to dine with Strauss, and showed him a libretto he had made from the great German classic, *Simplizius Simplicissimus*, by Christian Grimmelshausen. Léon's *Simplizius* was a serious story about the Thirty Years' War. It is hard to believe that Strauss immediately wanted it, but Léon, no fool, hinted he had given the libretto to an obscure composer, Alfred Zamara. Strauss immediately reacted in true Viennese operetta style: he said he would *have* to have the book. 'Léon's *Simplizius* is the most outstanding book I've seen lately . . . I say this, though I am no longer the naïve Jeany when I select my books,' he wrote to Lewy. In the long run Strauss was right about his enthusiasm for Victor Léon, who later wrote the libretto of *The Merry Widow*.

In 1886 Strauss went to St Petersburg once more where he conducted ten concerts, *Die Fledermaus* and *The Gipsy Baron*. A Moscow impresario offered him a great deal of money for two concerts there, and Strauss accepted. He was a rich man, but he now had delusions of getting poor. To Schnitzer he wrote, 'The royalties are getting smaller and I'll soon be broke. . . In Hamburg they no longer play *Gipsy Baron*. The book isn't "amusing"! The music is too "highbrow".' From Moscow he went back to St Petersburg and conducted once more in Pavlovsk.

Back in Vienna he wrote to Lewy, '*Simplizius* will be more amusing than *Gipsy Baron*. Instead of Hungarian rhythms I'll have the Viennese genre.' His nerves were getting worse, and he asked Priester to get him a dog for his estate at Schönau.

Our house is so secluded that it might attract criminals. . . . But the dog should be asked to differentiate between the proprietor and the thieves. . .

The experts who had predicted disaster for *The Gipsy Baron* now prophesied big success for *Simplizius*. They were wrong again. The premiere at the Theater an der Wien on 17 December 1887 was pretty dreadful. Strauss had got completely lost. *Simplizius* had neither the gay spirit of an operetta nor the pathos of an opera. During the premiere a gas flame set light to a chorister's hat, and there were cries of 'Fire!'. Some people, terrified by memories of the recent Ringtheater holocaust, jumped up from their seats. Panic seemed inevitable, but Strauss, who was conducting, with unusual self-possession lifted his baton and shouted to Josephi who sang the Hermit, 'Josephi, da capo!' The song was repeated, and calm was restored. 'Your wonderful music and your astonishing presence of mind have saved the lives of thousands,' Viktor Tilgner, the sculptor, wrote to Strauss the next day. But there was no help for *Simplizius*, even though Girardi was magnificent in the title role. Even with him in the cast the operetta closed after thirty performances. Strauss showed some wry humour when he wrote to his publisher to send him the entire *Simplizius* material. 'I don't want the cheese merchant to wrap his goods in my *Simplizius*.'

Strauss knew that he was well off – some said he was quite rich – but in his late years he was often obsessed by this recurrent fear of poverty. He had seen his father squander his money. He had lived through several crashes. He remembered the depression that followed the opening of the Vienna Exhibition of 1873, when rich men had become beggars overnight. Towards the end of his life he was conscious of the tragedy of his brother Eduard who had lost his considerable fortune through his son's speculation. All this made Strauss conservative in his investment policy. He put most of his money into property. Besides the two houses in Igelgasse, which formed the mansion, and the villa in Ischl, he owned four large apartment houses in Vienna's third and eighth districts, although he had long ago sold the country estate in Schönau because he identified it with Lili, his disastrous second wife. He owned few securities. In his estate the property amounted to over 800,000 guilders, his securities only to

The Strauss villa at Bad Ischl.

233

some 2,600 guilders. He shared his royalties with his librettists. In the case of *Gipsy Baron*, Strauss got 55 per cent, Schnitzer 45 per cent. Even so, he could still write to Priester, 'The royalties are getting smaller, and without royalties I shall be broke because I keep my houses for my own use instead of renting them for lots of money. I cannot help it though. It costs me a lot to work without being disturbed.' Privacy was getting expensive even then, but Strauss was exaggerating. Another time he complained to Priester:

. . . The day after tomorrow Hanslick and Brahms will dine here. They are used to eating well. Trout, crayfish, duck, geese, two desserts, and two different wines. Goodness, this is asking a lot from a composer who had three failures in succession!

And to Eduard he wrote in another bad moment, '. . . only let's not lose our sense of humour. If we no longer have anything, we shall all eat potatoes.'

17

'What a charming magician'

After Strauss retired from conducting and the active management of his orchestra – about at the time when he married Jetty – he devoted most of his energy to composing. People close to him knew that he was almost always mentally working, even when he was not in his study. He had regular work habits, even though he kept unorthodox hours. He loved to work late at night when everything was quiet around him. No one was permitted to be in his study or even nearby. During the long hectic nights when he wrote *Die Fledermaus* in Hietzing he would try out new ideas on his piano. Robert Fischhof, a young boy living in the adjoining house who was quite a good musician, would listen through the wall. During a visit to the Strauss home with his father, Fischhof sat down and played some of the still top-secret tunes for Strauss, who was quite upset, and had his study moved to a room where no one could listen from the outside.

He did not need much sleep. After breakfast he would disappear into his study again. Once in a while he might walk into the adjoining billiard room and practice for a while, but the remote expression in his eyes indicated that he was still very much with his music, and was not to be disturbed. After a leisurely lunch he might go back to the study again. He was always working, even on Sundays and holidays; he enjoyed it.

Late in the afternoon friends would come for a game of cards. Strauss used to say that the only time when he was not thinking of his music was when he had to concentrate on his game of tarock, but even then an absent-minded look might suddenly come into his eyes. Friends always understood and kept quiet. Even so, although he did not mind criticism as a composer, he was really hurt when they teased him about mistakes at tarock. In 1886, when he was offered much money and expenses for himself and Adele to conduct concerts in St Petersburg, Pavlovsk and Moscow, he stipulated in the contract

RIGHT A note from Strauss
inviting Ludwig Eisenberg to
play tarock at Bad Ischl.

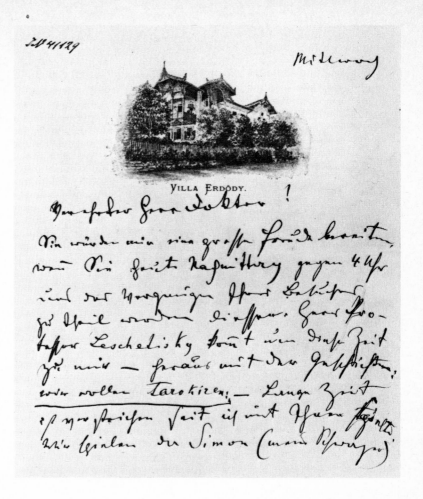

OPPOSITE Although so different
as men and musicians, Brahms
and Strauss had a deep respect
for each other.

'expenses for a third man to be sure of my daily tarock game'. Once he
wrote to a friend from Ischl, 'Except for playing tarock I do only a
little work in the morning, writing notes. . . .'

His friends in his latter years were men with whom he could relax.
They were not sophisticated. There was no intellectual talk; there
was rarely any talk about music. Strauss, the most famous of them all,
was acutely aware of his station in musical life. He knew that he was
'more popular' and much better known the world over than Brahms.
(The result of a poll in 1890 was that the 'most popular' people in
Europe were 1 Queen Victoria, 2 Bismarck, 3 Johann Strauss.) But
Strauss also knew that Brahms was in the stratosphere of composing,
compared to himself.

Brahms liked the relaxed atmosphere in the Strauss home – in
Vienna or in Ischl – and he came often in his last years. There was no
formality. Strauss's idea of a *gemütlich* home was to make it a per-

236

ABOVE Strauss playing cards with his friends. Adele stands behind him.

manent coffee-house for his friends and himself. Adele might have had more elegant ideas, but she was wise enough not to insist. Instead of elaborate dinners served by liveried footmen there would be sausages (the ones called Frankfurter in Vienna and Wiener in Frankfurt), and wine from nearby Gumpoldskirchen. Strauss himself loved a Meerschaum pipe, but there were fine cigars for the friends.

They were a small, congenial group; they shared his preference for the simple pleasures of life. Viktor Tilgner, a genuine 'Old-Viennese', a well-known sculptor; Ludwig Bösendorfer, another local 'original'; Theodor Leschetitzky, the pianist and teacher; Alfred Grünfeld, the concert pianist; the composer Karl Goldmark, from Hungary, very famous in Vienna after the success of his *Queen of Sheba*; Ignatz Schnitzer; Gustav Lewy, classmate, adviser and publisher; Theodor Leschetizky, the noted piano teacher; Ludwig Ganghofer, the playwright; and Ludwig Dóczi. Sometimes Brahms and the conductor Nikisch would join them. And there might also be Strauss's father-in-law and his brother Eduard.

238

In his younger years Strauss had loved people and parties, and going out and staying up late. As he got older, he rarely left his home. He said he liked being only with people he was fond of, 'but that may be my fault'. His friends would never talk about him or his work – things he disliked. Compliments made him feel uncomfortable. He had never considered himself a particularly good conductor; he thought Eduard was a more popular one in Vienna. When he did some shopping and had no money to pay – he often forgot his wallet – he would say, 'My name is Strauss, I am the brother of Edi Strauss,' as though he expected this would establish his credit. It did, too.

Fritz Lange writes, 'Strauss was a civilized *homme du monde*, charming and kind, the type of the elegant Viennese. He was not jealous, never expressed hard criticism of others. When he was asked to autograph a printed card with his picture and words "Meister Strauss", he would always cross out "Meister".'

There are still a few old people in Vienna whose parents knew and admired Johann Strauss. They describe him as a fascinating artist. His biographer Eisenberg calls him 'the prototype of the dashing Viennese'. Both Strauss and the Emperor went to the same tailor, who summed them up as 'Two difficult customers who know what they want, never complain, and pay their bills promptly'.

As a composer Strauss was understood and often praised by the three heads of the horrible hydra – the public, the critics, his own peers. He remains an all-time master practitioner of mass hypnotism,

ABOVE The back of a menu signed by Strauss and his friends.

ABOVE The back of a menu signed by Strauss and his friends.

RIGHT Strauss and Adele, with her daughter standing beside the carriage, outside the villa at Bad Ischl.

OPPOSITE Some of Strauss's
friends and contemporaries:
TOP LEFT Ludwig Ganghofer;
TOP RIGHT Gustav Lewy;
BOTTOM LEFT Richard Wagner;
BOTTOM RIGHT A cartoon of
Arthur Nikisch.

but he used his power to make people happy and to disarm his
critics. In Vienna Hugo Wolf was ignored, Wagner was ridiculed,
Bruckner and later Mahler were misunderstood – but Strauss was
accepted. Most criticism of his stage works was directed against the
impossible libretti, and often mingled with regret that Strauss wasted
his beautiful melodies on such silly stories.

He also had the respect of those he respected most, the great
composers of his time. 'It may sound paradoxical but Strauss, the
waltz king, was the first to pave the way for Wagner in Vienna,'
writes Fritz Lange. His mother was one of the early Wagnerians in
Vienna, at a time when Eduard Hanslick and many Establishment
critics were violently against Wagner. Strauss inherited her enthusiasm. He performed selections from Wagner's early operas before they
were given at the Kärnthnertortheater. When the Vienna rehearsals
of *Tristan und Isolde* were stopped after seventeen months (and after
Hanslick had declared that the work was 'unperformable'), Strauss
and his orchestra played selections from all three acts at the Volksgarten. Wagner was not charitable towards his fellow composers, and
liked conveniently to forget favours that other people had done for
him, but he did not forget Strauss. On his sixty-third birthday he was
listening to an amateur orchestra in Bayreuth conducted by Anton
Seidl. Suddenly Wagner got up, took the baton and conducted his
favourite Strauss waltz *Wine, Women and Song*. During the difficult
negotiations with the owner of the site where Wagner later built his
villa Wahnfried, Wagner sat down at the piano and played a Strauss
waltz – to calm down or to please the property-owner who probably
had little love for Wagner's own music. At a banquet, Wagner once
tossed off a toast 'to our classics, from Mozart to Strauss'. He called
Strauss 'the most musical brain I've ever known'.

Hans von Bülow, who first conducted *Tristan* and was one of the
great conductors of his time, heard Strauss in 1872 in Baden-Baden
and wrote, 'What a charming magician! His compositions, which he
conducted himself, gave me one of the most stimulating musical
pleasures in a long time. Strauss is one of the few colleagues whom I
admire without reservation. . . . From his performances one can learn
things for the Ninth Symphony and for the *Pathétique*.' A few years
later he wrote to Marie von Bülow, 'Delibes' *Lakmé* disappoints me.
He should have composed ballets, just as Strauss should have stayed
with his waltzes and polkas.' In an essay *The Public and the Critics*,
Bülow mentions 'the dramatic masterpiece, *Carmen*, highly admired
by Brahms and by Wagner, who also agreed on their love for Johann
Strauss's waltzes'.

'Brahms, who used to treat the Viennese school with merciless
sarcasm, would never say an offending word to Strauss, not as a joke

240

even,' writes Max Kalbeck, Brahms's biographer. When Adele Strauss, following a current fashion, asked Brahms to autograph her fan, Brahms wrote the first bars of *The Blue Danube*, and underneath signed, 'Unfortunately not by – Johannes Brahms'. On 26 June 1888, Brahms wrote from a Swiss holiday in Thun to 'Meister' Strauss that he had heard *Die Fledermaus* in Berne. There were not many composers whom Brahms would honour with 'Meister'.

Brahms admired Strauss for his very special talent. Brahms also wrote fine waltzes but he had no illusions that they were Viennese waltzes and that they could be danced.

For his part Strauss was somewhat awed by the bearded romanticist from North Germany who was so completely un-Viennese, so reticent and withdrawn. In his later years he saw much of Brahms who was often invited there by Adele. Brahms, who rarely relaxed in the company of women, seemed to like Adele, but Strauss never quite understood the solemn, serious symphonist who could be cheerful only in his music and was considered an eccentric in Vienna. The Viennese instinctively distrust solemnity. There is an atavistic belief that such people have something to hide. But Strauss, often puzzled by Brahms the man, understood Brahms the composer, and dedicated to him one of his great, late waltzes, *Seid umschlungen, Millionen*.

Once Brahms said to Strauss, 'Imagine if we had failed with our best things – you with *Fledermaus* and I with my *Requiem*!' Strauss nodded. 'Yes, Herr Doktor. We two were not always lucky. One always has problems with that damn music.' When Fritz Simrock in 1891 had an offer from America – 120,000 guilders if Strauss would conduct a few concerts – Strauss wrote, 'Brahms tells me that the 120,000 guilders would be very pleasant, but not the journey. Nothing but collisions. Too much fog over the Atlantic. I prefer the fog over Vienna.' That made it final, since Simrock was also the publisher of Brahms.

Strauss loved to hear his waltzes played by Brahms on the piano. One evening at his home, after he had played for his friends, Strauss asked Brahms for a fugue. Brahms began to improvise and gradually introduced melodies from *The Blue Danube* with artful variations. When he stopped, there were a few moments of silence, and then Strauss said wistfully, 'Yes, those are my waltzes . . . I've never heard them so beautifully played.'

Bruckner had no use for Brahms, but he too liked Strauss. 'I like a Strauss waltz better than a whole symphony by Brahms,' he would say. This surprised some people who said that Bruckner and Strauss lived in different worlds. Yet occasionally Bruckner and Strauss approached one another in their music. Bruckner becomes almost Straussian in the scherzos of some of his symphonies; Strauss takes us to the gates of heaven in his *Sphärenklänge Waltz*.

Bruckner was trying to communicate with God. Strauss wanted to reach the hearts of his fellow human beings. The dionysian was terrified at the very thought of death, but this held no horror for Bruckner. As musicians, however, they understood one another. Bruckner once spent an hour standing behind the door of the Musikverein Hall, listening to Strauss as he sat at a piano on the platform of the empty hall and improvised. Strauss sent Bruckner a telegram after the first performance of his Seventh Symphony.

They rarely met. Bruckner – mild, religious and going around in slippers – was not exactly Adele Strauss's idea of the ideal guest for the house in Igelgasse. Once she invited Bruckner to a *Backhendl* (fried chicken) party shortly after Bruckner had returned from his pilgrimmage to Bayreuth. It would be fun, she thought, to listen to Bruckner, always with one foot in heaven, telling them about Wagner's private heaven. They were not disappointed. Bruckner's involuntary brand of humour made them laugh for hours.

Anton Bruckner in a silhouette by Böhler.

18
The Emperor Waltz

OPPOSITE Dommayer's Casino in Hietzing where Strauss had his first triumph in 1844. A watercolour by Richard Moswe.

In 1888 Austria-Hungary celebrated another jubilee. On 2 December it was forty years since the young Franz Joseph had been crowned emperor. He was only fifty-eight, but to the people he seemed much older. He lived in Olympian isolation, and the only people he saw regularly were the members of his immediate family and his mistress, Katharina Schratt, whom he had met two years earlier. Nevertheless he was revered in Vienna for the dignity with which he carried the burden of what everybody knew was an unhappy private life. It was an open secret in Vienna that his marriage was a complete failure. Elisabeth, beautiful and not interested in her duties as an Empress, would go away for months, to Hungary and Greece, with friends. Or she might be riding and hunting in England and Ireland. She was not popular in Vienna, although the Crown Prince Rudolph was – especially with the liberal bourgeoisie. One of his intimates was Moritz Szeps, an editor of *Neues Wiener Tagblatt*. And even people who liked Rudolph wished that he would get along with the Emperor.

It was against this background that Strauss made a personal contribution to the jubilee when he wrote one of his most inspired masterpieces, the *Kaiserwalzer (Emperor Waltz)*, Opus 437. In earlier years, when Strauss was still *Hofballmusikdirektor*, he had seen the Emperor at one of the ceremonial balls that Franz Joseph attended. There was the Court Ball, which was only for the court itself, the highest civilian and military dignitaries and the recipients of Imperial decorations; and the Ball at Court, which was for members of the diplomatic corps and the high aristocracy. The Emperor would remain graceful and distant, and he would soon leave. Ordinary mortals rarely talked to him. The Viennese might see him for a short moment when he was driven from the Hofburg in the Inner City to Schönbrunn, or during the change of the guard. He spent his summers in Bad Ischl.

OVERLEAF 'Feste' by Gause, showing the Emperor Franz Joseph at a ball.

244

HIETZING, ETABLISSEMENT "DOSMAYER"

RICARD MOT

Strauss had bought a villa there that had once belonged to Countess Marie Erdödy, the friend of Beethoven.

Strauss, the one-time revolutionary who had played the *Marseillaise* at the barricades in 1848, had come full circle when he wrote the *Emperor Waltz*. It was the quintessence of his devotion, sympathy and sadness for the Emperor. He expressed in his music exactly what millions of people felt about Franz Joseph. He said it poetically and prophetically in the haunting undertones, and once more the poet was right. The worst was yet to come. A few weeks after his father's jubilee, on 29 January 1889, Crown Prince Rudolph shot Marie Vetsera and himself in the bedroom of his small hunting lodge at Mayerling, in the Wienerwald. And a few years later, in 1898, Empress Elisabeth was assassinated by an anarchist at Territet, near Geneva. And Katherina Schratt withdrew from him at a time when he might have needed a sympathetic friend and someone to talk to. Schratt never talked. She turned down fabulous offers for her memories.

OPPOSITE The monument to Strauss in the City Park, erected in 1923.

ABOVE A portrait of Marie Vetsera, mistress to Crown Prince Rudolph (BELOW), which was found on the body of the Prince after he had shot Marie and himself in 1889.

The title *Emperor Waltz* had been supplied by Fritz Simrock, the publisher. It has no dedication, even though the title page of the first edition bears the Austrian crown. Yet there is no doubt for whom Strauss wrote it. William Ritter, the French musicologist, in *Les Derniers Oeuvres de Johann Strauss* calls the *Emperor Waltz* 'the most beautiful flower that has come during the century from the Strauss dynasty in Vienna'. Ritter places the great waltzes that Strauss wrote in his late years 'beside the works of Beethoven, Wagner and Bruckner'. After a beautiful introduction, 74-bars long, somewhat reminiscent of the officers' march in *Così fan Tutte*, the waltz begins *Ben legato ed espressivo* in what Ritter calls 'le grand style des allures lentes'. The second part, by contrast, is joyful and vivacious, and in the coda Strauss once more looks back and pays homage to the lonely man in the Hofburg. Paul Lindau, the writer, later wrote to Strauss, 'I am not exaggerating when I tell you that I feel that nothing has been written since the days of Schubert which can be compared to the first part of your *Emperor Waltz*, with its true melody and innocent beauty. In the first sixteen bars there is more genuine music than in many operas that last a whole evening and leave the head and the heart empty.'

Chronologically and musically the history of the Strauss dynasty remains closely connected with the late history of the Habsburgs. The first Johann Strauss was born in 1804. That year Franz II, the German Emperor, assumed the crown as hereditary emperor of Austria, calling himself Franz I. Two years later, with the resignation of Franz II, the Holy Roman Empire ceased to exist.

Johann Strauss the second died in 1899. Franz Decsey quotes an

anonymous court official who later said, 'Emperor Franz Joseph reigned in reality only until the death of Johann Strauss.' Actually Franz Joseph I died in 1916, but by the end of the nineteenth century the centrifugal forces were beginning to tear apart the Habsburg monarchy. Although many people refused to acknowledge it, the empire was doomed. It survived its musical poet by only two decades. Strauss was one of the few bridge builders. The Hungarians loved his *Gipsy Baron*, the Czechs and Poles heard their motives in some of his polkas and waltzes. A chronicler said – and with truth – that 'the music of Strauss poured honey into the Austrian powder keg'.

Strauss still had the ambition of writing a true opera. To his brother-in-law Josef Simon he wrote, 'The operetta librettos nowadays have no touch of poetry; they are dull and trivial. If this goes on, people are going to say, "Strauss ought to write operas".' One who kept saying it was Adele. Had he not written the greatest waltzes and fine operettas? In Vienna a composer was awarded his musical crown only after being performed at the Court Opera. The question was, could Strauss write opera?

He met Ludwig Dóczi, a high administrative official who had been brought from Budapest to Vienna by Count Julius Andrassy, the Foreign Minister. Dóczi was also a successful playwright. At the Burgtheater people had been amused by his comedy, *The Kiss*. The mixture of bureaucrat and literary man had not been unusual in Vienna since the days of Grillparzer. Dóczi suggested to Strauss a libretto based on the ballad *Ritter Pasman* by the great Hungarian poet János Arany (1817–82). Strauss at once considered the idea perfect for an opera. He liked the Hungarian setting: after all it had been so successful in *The Gipsy Baron*. Contracts were signed, and Dóczi started to write. A Hungarian king falls in love with the beautiful wife of Ritter (Knight) Pasman, his vassal. The complications of honour and love are confounded by a court jester. The drama has moments of romantic beauty and long stretches of boredom, and Simrock later said he would have preferred 'one new waltz'.

However, Strauss and Simrock were often fighting. In 1891 Strauss wrote to Priester, 'No wonder I'm suffering from nervous pains. Herr Simrock, never satisfied, continues to irritate me. . . .' Simrock was not the only sceptic. When Ignatz Schnitzer said jokingly, after looking at the score of *Ritter Pasman*, 'At least, you can sing, as Valentin in *Faust*, "I die as a soldier and brave"', Strauss almost broke off with his friend.

Wilhelm Jahn accepted *Ritter Pasman* for the Court Opera, and Strauss was absolutely happy as he sat in the darkened auditorium listening to the rehearsals. Dóczi later told Procházka, the Strauss biographer, that on one of these occasions he had sat next to Strauss.

TANZWEISEN-ABEND
UNTER DER DEVISE
„WIEN IM DREIVIERTELTAKT!"
GROSSER MUSIKVEREINSSAAL
16. NOVEMBER 1912.

The orchestra played beautifully, and Strauss had his eyes closed. Afterwards he said, 'Now I've heard my music. This is what I've hoped for all my life. I don't care what they are going to say.'

Strauss was no fool: he knew that it is the comedian's hopeless ambition to play Hamlet. They said exactly what he'd expected. The premiere at the Court Opera was only received with respect on 1 January 1892. Strauss was sixty-seven, the great Viennese Meister, a symbol of the Viennese city, like St Stephen's Cathedral. For weeks there had been talk of a 'sensation'. The *Neue Freie Presse* wrote that tickets were selling for ten times their face value. Yet the critics remained cool. Speidel characteristically wrote that the applause had been strongest after the waltz aria in the second act, and the ballet in the third act. Hanslick said, 'We missed in this higher sphere our old, beloved Johann Strauss,' and called the ballet music, 'the crown jewel of the score'. Strauss later said that 'people believe there should be no slow tempo in a Strauss opera'. The opera was given only nine times in Vienna, but it was also seen in Prague, Berlin and Brussels. Strauss was so pleased with the Prague production under Angelo Neumann and so exhilarated by its reception that he seriously considered buying a house there. But even in Prague the success of *Ritter Pasman* was short-lived, and Strauss admitted in a letter to his brother Eduard, 'I confess that the opera is already gone, a thing of the past for me.'

Strauss never quite recovered from this disappointment so late in his life. He wrote four operettas after this: *Fürstin Ninetta (Princess Ninetta)*, premiered 10 January 1893; *Jabuka*, 12 October 1894; *Waldmeister*, 4 December 1895; and *Die Göttin der Vernunft (The*

OPPOSITE Theo Zasche's drawings of the major characters from the Strauss operettas.

The cast list of *Ritter Pasman* at the Court Opera.

Goddess of Reason), 13 March 1897. The reaction of public and critics alike was always respectful and sad. One did not criticize Strauss anymore; it was just not done. Fortunately there was always a waltz one could praise; there was Strauss himself conducting the overture which gave the people a chance to cheer him; and there was Girardi, so that no evening was a complete loss. Perhaps the audience was always hoping for the miracle of another *Fledermaus*. If so, the hope was a forlorn one.

Still, there were happy moments. Emperor Franz Joseph I came to the Theater an der Wien for the premiere of *Princess Ninetta*. He had not been there for twenty-five years, although there had been periods when he went to his favourite, the Burgtheater, almost every night.

The Theater an der Wien had recently installed electric lighting. The performance lasted long because many numbers had to be repeated. After the second act, Johann Strauss was summoned to the imperial box. The Emperor was graceful and distant, as always. 'Your music doesn't get older, and neither do you,' he told the ex-revolutionary, ex-Catholic. Strauss mumbled something, and the Emperor smiled. 'You haven't changed. Amazing, really, I haven't seen you for years, and you seem the same.'

The following year, 1894, was the fiftieth anniversary of Strauss's debut at Dommayer's. The popular gossip paper, *Neues Wiener Journal*, had a good idea: instead of writing a boring appreciation they sent their reporters to famous contemporaries to get their opinions. Alexandre Dumas, son, called Strauss 'a god who masters passions'. The eighty-three-year-old Ambroise Thomas, composer of *Mignon*, talked about 'ce cher, ce gentil Strauss', and remembered that *ce cher* Cherubini (not known to be *gentil*) had 'applauded like a paid claqueur' when Father Strauss had performed in Paris.

Emile Zola told the reporter that even after writing twenty-two novels he did not know how to express his admiration for 'Maître Strauss'. 'He is lucky – he has shown the world how beautiful it can be. I told the world how awful it can be.' Zola had said more in a few words than most writers on æsthetics had. And Sarah Bernhardt said she wished she were in Vienna so she could embrace Strauss 'and kiss him, kiss him. . . . That's the only way a woman should show her homage.'

There was another long, hard day – 14 October. Civic societies, musical groups, the members of the Vienna Philharmonic, the Military Kapellmeister of Vienna, artists, friends, celebrities. Strauss had promised to conduct part of a concert of the Philharmoniker, but at the last moment he wrote to Schnitzer,

I beg you to make Kalbeck and Dömpke forget about the concert at the Musikverein. . . . If I still played the violin, I could at least show how to do a crisp bow stroke, but to perform a waltz with a baton in the hand seems silly. . . .

That night the Court Opera paid its homage not by a performance of *Ritter Pasman*, but by having its ballet dance to *The Blue Danube*. Strauss had been hiding 'in the rear of a box', but when the applause forced him to stand up, he appeared 'pale but happy'.

255

WALZER: Ich denke gern zurück.

Zum Jubiläum des Walzerkönigs.

19
'One day one must go'

A deep malaise runs through three generations of the Strauss family. It begins with the probable suicide of Franz Strauss, a few years after his son Johann was born. It continues through the life of the first Johann Strauss, who remained ambitious, restless and unhappy to his death. He never reconciled himself with the success of his eldest son. He did not understand that the younger Johann admired him and wanted to emulate his father. Today it is a fact that the success of the son revived the music and the fame of the father.

The father's tragedy repeated itself with Josef, his second son and the most gifted member of this musical family. Josef went through long spells of depression and was convinced that he would not live long. Just like his father he worked too hard, and ruined his health. He suffered from fainting spells and painful migraine attacks; some medical authorities think he suffered from a tumour of the brain.

Even Johann, the most balanced of the brothers, had a touch of the family malaise. Behind the façade of success and glitter there was an insecure man, human and weak and lovable, always loyal to the people around him. Artist's jealousy and intrigue was alien to him. He was happy with the success of his brother Josef, and later of Eduard. He had more self-discipline than his father, but there were moments when he needed a drink to calm his anxieties. Although he lived in an era that seems calm in retrospect, he was often under stress and there was always the fear of tomorrow's review in the paper. He was a great composer, but he often had to compose *against* somebody. Early in his career he was compelled by circumstances beyond his control to compete with his father. Later he had to prove himself against Offenbach and then against Suppé and Millöcker. As he got older he had health problems. In 1893 he wrote to Eduard:

I would have come for a visit but my neuralgia and my lung catarrh don't permit me to leave the house. . . . And now there is my old fear of a return of the influenza that made me ill six months last year. . . .

OPPOSITE A poster for the fifteenth anniversary of Strauss's first appearance at Dommayer's Casino, with pictures of Johann, his father and brothers.

Strauss at Bad Ischl in 1898, the year before his death.

After the excitement of the fifty-year jubilee Strauss thanked his brother Eduard ('Your orchestra performed magnificently last Sunday at the Large Musikverein Hall') and confesses:

Thank God these days are gone. My nerves are not made of iron to stand such a strain.... My eyes are weak from writing notes all these years because I wrote mostly at night. I see everything double. If I take a toothpick, I see two in front of me. Should I have the tragedy of getting blind, I'll shoot myself. Not to be able to write music anymore would mean no more joy in life....

Strauss, however, had not lost the ability to write music. He still had ideas most of the time, but he may have lost touch with the changing times or – more probably – did not choose to be aware of them.

There had been strong social changes in Vienna within a decade. Around the Gürtel the last fortifications, put up during the Turkish siege, were razed, and Greater Vienna was created. Strauss musically sanctioned the event by writing the *Gross Wien Waltz* for the Concordia Ball in 1890. A few weeks later, on 1 May, workers, their wives and children marched in the Prater, singing and carrying red flags: it was the first successful May Day demonstration in Europe. Stefan Zweig remembers in *Die Welt von Gestern (The World of Yesterday)* that his parents forbade their children 'to go out in the street on this day of terror, which might see Vienna in flames'. The historian Josef Redlich noticed a new class-consciousness. 'The feudal aristocracy at the top broke away from the Jewish financial circles. Social democracy became the enemy of both. The new society did away with the old distinctions. The popular concert began to compete with the exclusive Philharmonic concerts, and the Volksoper challenged the privileged Court Opera.' Ilsa Barea writes of 'a phosphorescent glitter about Vienna that came from the irrevocable decay of the foundations on which the capital rested'.

Strauss cut himself off from the outside world. Only a few intimates were admitted to his house in Igelgasse or to the villa in Ischl, where he worked in the garden and played tarock.

When Gustav Mahler became director of the Court Opera in 1897, he toyed with the idea of reviving *Ritter Pasman*. Mahler wrote to Ludwig Dóczi:

I gather that the production didn't quite satisfy your intentions and those of Meister Strauss. It is strange and a recurrent fact in the history of all new productions that the *Herren Direktoren* and producer consider the presence of the authors as superfluous and disturbing ... I assure you that ... in the case of a revival of *Pasman* at the Court Opera I would insist on your co-operation and Strauss's....

258

Böhler's silhouette entitled 'Johannes, Johann, Hans', showing Brahms, Strauss and Richter playing cards.

Ritter Pasman was not taken into the repertory, but Mahler accepted one of the last things Strauss wrote, the ballet *Aschenbrödel (Cinderella)*. The idea had come from Hanslick, who later wrote, 'The beautiful ballet music in the opera *Pasman* renewed in me an old wish: Strauss ought to write a ballet for the Court Opera. For a long time he refused, but then he suddenly set up a prize for the best idea for a merry ballet. . . . A deluge of some eight hundred scenarios was sent in. Strauss selected a modern version of the old Cinderella fairy tale.' Strauss never saw the production at the Opera: *Cinderella* was performed ten years after his death.

On the afternoon of Whit Monday, 22 May 1899, Strauss was to conduct *Die Fledermaus* at the Court Opera. He was given an ovation as he took his place in the pit, and again after the overture. It was noticed that he then stepped down, and was replaced by another conductor. He had felt dizzy, and his shirt was soaked with perspiration. After being driven home he felt better, and Bösendorfer and Leschetizky arrived for their game of tarock. After a short rest Strauss joined them. That night he worked on some revisions that Mahler requested on *Cinderella*.

Strauss and Adele (LEFT) out walking in the Prater.

Two days later Strauss and Adele attended a fashion show at the Prater. It was a warm day, but there were sudden gusts of cool wind, as often in Vienna, and Strauss felt unwell again. Once home he had to go to bed because he was feverish. After a day or so he felt better, and got up to welcome Mark Twain who had come to pay his respects. He was Strauss's last visitor. Twelve days later Twain wrote to Adele:

When I talked and smoked with Mr Strauss in your house, he seemed his old self – alert, quick, brilliant in speech, wearing the grace of his indestructible youth. . . . It seems impossible that he is gone! I am grateful that I was privileged to have that pleasant meeting with him, and it will remain a gracious memory with me.

The next day he felt worse again. Two days later his wife called Dr Lederer, the family physician, who consulted with Professor Hermann Nothnagel. Their diagnosis was pneumonia and pleurisy. Adele implored them not to tell Strauss the truth. They said it was 'a bad cold', but Strauss who had been terrified all his life of death and dying, now sensed the truth. On the afternoon of 2 June Adele and

her daughter Alice sat by his bedside. Strauss was dozing. Suddenly he opened his eyes, and sang softly, '*Brüderlein fein . . . es muss geschieden sein*' ('. . . one day one must go'). His former music teacher, Joseph Drechsler, had written the melancholy song.

Later Strauss asked Adele for the *Cinderella* score, saying that there was still some work to be done on it. She told him not to worry, to try to sleep. He kissed her hand, smiled and closed his eyes. He had always been afraid of death, but he was asleep when death at last came. At 4.15 in the afternoon of 3 June his heart stopped beating.

Less than one hour after Strauss died everybody in town seems to have known. At the Volksgarten – where Strauss and his father had lived through many triumphs – Eduard Kremser was conducting a benefit concert to raise money for the projected monument of Lanner and Father Strauss in the Döbling Cemetery. Somebody came in and said something to Kremser. He stopped the music and whispered to the musicians, and then the audience heard the *pianissimo* tremolo of the introduction to *The Blue Danube*. Everybody got up. They understood. Many were crying.

The Volksgarten, where the playing of the Blue Danube in the middle of a concert gave the news of the death of Strauss.

Three days later – on 6 June – Strauss was buried. The funeral procession started from the house in Igelgasse. In accordance with a Viennese tradition the cortège walked slowly around the buildings where he had had his moments of glory: the Theater an der Wien, the Musikverein, the Court Opera. Many houses along the route were draped in black. The sun was shining, but in accordance with another Viennese tradition the mayor had ordered 'that the street lights be turned on, at the expense of the City, in the streets passed by the funeral cortège'. He also ordered that the City councillors join the procession, 'tails, black tie'.

Strauss's violin was carried on a velvet cushion by a member of his orchestra, walking behind the coffin. H. E. Jacob, who was then a nine-year-old boy, much later wrote that 'It was as though they had carried all the gardens of Vienna out to the Central Cemetery.' Strauss was buried in a section reserved for the immortals – next to Beethoven, Schubert and Brahms. The chorus of the Singverein sang Brahms's *Fahr wohl* by way of musical farewell.

Strauss left piles of musical manuscripts behind – sketches and completed pieces, long-forgotten unpublished waltzes, polkas, quad-rilles, melodies he had jotted down and never used. The material was entirely unsorted, and Strauss had never bothered to examine it carefully, even though when director Janner of the Carltheater asked Strauss for a new operetta in the spring of 1899, he had sug-gested that possibly 'some older material' might be used so Strauss would not have to work too hard.

Strauss never did anything about this idea, but after his death Victor Léon, the librettist of *Simplizius*, and Leo Stein concocted a book to fit the hitherto unused music – an amusing period story of the time of the Congress of Vienna (1814). There were scenes in Hietzing where Strauss had lived; there was a big ball scene (the librettists had learned the lesson of *Die Fledermaus*); mistaken identities; confusion confounded. The whole thing had a very good title – *Wiener Blut*. (It defies English translation: *Viennese Blood* would be all wrong. The idea is that to have Viennese blood in one's veins makes one courageous and strong.)

Strauss had known of this idea a few weeks before his death and had suggested Adolf Müller, an able musician and conductor at the Theater an der Wien, as the arranger of the material for the projected operetta. Müller went through crates of manuscripts and musical ideas jotted down on all kinds of paper, and skilfully put together a pastiche which proved both his respect for Strauss and his own sound technique. The premiere of *Wiener Blut* took place on 25 October 1899, a few months after Strauss's death, and everybody had pre-dicted a terrific success. They had always loved Strauss's music, and

ABOVE Böhler's silhouettes of
Strauss conducting waltzes in
heaven. Brahms and Mozart are
among the dancers.

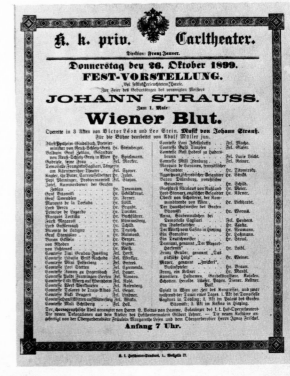

Cast list of *Wiener Blut* in 1899.

this would be a sort of requiem, the sentimental sort of affair that the Viennese always like.

Nevertheless *Wiener Blut* was a flop. The critics complained it sounded 'much too familiar'. After a short run it was taken off. Jauner, so depressed that he almost had a nervous breakdown, told Adele he just could not understand why *Wiener Blut* had failed. Three years later, however, the management of the Theater an der Wien had a feud with Alexander Girardi, and a show was needed at short notice. They produced *Wiener Blut* once more, and it was an outstanding success. The operetta survived, and is now performed as a 'genuine' Strauss work all over the world. In its wake various teams of librettists and arrangers put together five more posthumous operettas from Strauss material. None had the success of *Wiener Blut*.

After Strauss's death Hanslick wrote that 'the most original Viennese genius' had gone.

His melodic invention was inexhaustible. His rhythms were forever alive and changing. His harmony and form were pure.

He called one of his most beautiful waltzes *Liebeslieder* [love songs]. But all of them were love songs – intimate tales of a shy courtship, of exhilarating happiness, and often in between a bittersweet tinge of melancholy....

Long ago Strauss had said in the Preface to the Collected Works of his father:

Not for one moment he had the ambition to stand on the pedestal of great art. But *his* art banished many worries, smoothed many wrinkles, gave people joy in life – comforted, delighted, elated so many of them. This is why they will always remember him.

When the son wrote these words, he was more famous – and more modest – than his father had ever been. And he could not have written a finer memorial for himself.

Acknowledgments

The author's thanks are due to Professor Dr Fritz Racek, editor of the Collected Works of Johann Strauss; Professor Hanns Jäger-Sunstenau, historian and archivist of the Vienna City Hall Library; Professor Willi Boskovsky; to the officials of Vienna's National Library; to Mosco Carner (*The Waltz*); and to Strauss's former biographers, particularly Ernst Decsey who understood him best.

Photographs and illustrations were supplied or are reproduced by kind permission of the following: Bildarchiv d. Öst. National-bibliothek 19, 22, 30/1, 33, 34/2, 36, 37, 41, 46, 52/1, 58, 60, 63, 64, 80, 80–1, 90, 99, 110, 111, 121, 125, 137, 140, 142, 150, 156, 162, 171, 173, 179, 183, 200, 204, 208, 214, 220, 223, 227/1, 227/2, 227/3, 238, 239/1, 241/1, 241/2, 241/3, 253, 258, 263; Cooper Bridgeman Library *69*; Mary Evans Picture Library 53/2; Fotostudio Otto *87, 190–1*; Francoise Foliot 169; John Freeman 54; Glasgow Art Gallery and Museum 182; The Granger Collection, New York 177/1; Historisches Museum der Stadt Wien 8, *25, 26–7,* 28, 30/2, *35,* 38, 44, 57, 70, 76, 81, *88,* 93/2, 117, *123, 124,* 138, *146,* 157/1, 157/2, *163, 164,* 186/1, 186/2, 196, 197, *210–11, 212,* 215, 216, 221, 229, 239/2, *245,* 253, 256, 260; Erich Lessing–Magnum photos *66/1, 66/2, 133, 145, 189/1, 189/2, 248*; Lord's Gallery *192*; Mansell Collection 72, 118; Photo Hachette 203; Photo Meyer 10, 11, 40, *134–5,* 147, 160/1; Popperfoto 71, 241/4, 243, 249/1, 249/2, 251, 254, 261; Radio Times Hulton Picture Library 44, 194; Strauss Collection of Robert Rogers (photographs by Douglas Allen Photography, Bridgewater) 13, 34/1, 67, 68, 76/2, 86, 114, 126, 129, 130, *136,* 143, 152, 155, 172, 177/2, 188, 193, 201, *209/1, 209/2,* 218, 230, 231, 233, 259, Victoria and Albert Museum 148; Roger Viollet 48, 52/2, 65, 168; Votava 109, 165, 264; Wiener Stadtbibliothek 16, 17, 43, 53/1, 75, 93/1, 98, 120, 154, 158, 160/2, 199, 216.

Numbers in italics indicate colour plates.
Picture research by Andra Nelki.

266

Index